To the Grand Haven Christian School community.
Keep praying. God's answered across all your 144 years.

Pray daily for your school.

Miller, Nelson.

Crown Management, LLC – March 2024

1527 Pineridge Drive
Grand Haven, MI 49417
USA

ISBN-13: 979-8-89292-841-0

All Rights Reserved
© 2024 Crown Management, LLC

Table of Prayers

Accountability, 4/5
Accounting, 4/3
Advent, 12/4, 12/24
Adversary, 11/23
Administrators, 3/23
Aides, 1/30
Anxiety, 2/17
Application, 11/29
Apprenticeships, 5/8
Architects, 10/27
Art, 11/17
Athletics, 4/25
Ascent, 2/10
Bible, 9/27
Bless God, 4/9
Blessing, 12/20
Board members, 10/16
Board officers, 4/12
Board recruiting, 2/25
Board unity, 2/18
Board wisdom, 12/12
Boundaries, 5/23
Boys and Girls, 10/14
Build in struggle, 11/26
Building, 12/16
Building design, 2/15
Building fund, 10/28
Burial, 3/30
Care, 9/11
Christ education, 11/21
Church neighbor, 12/14
Citizenship, 5/12
City relationship, 2/7
Classroom aides, 10/18
Clear the temple, 3/26
Collaboration, 10/6
Coming year, 12/27
Commitment, 3/5
Committees, 11/4
Community, 10/7
Company, 5/24
Compassion, 9/10
Confession, 1/5, 1/3
Conscience, 1/31

Consent, 2/27
Construction, 9/6
Conviction, 2/26
Core beliefs, 3/24
Courage, 3/17
Cultivation, 11/28
Culture, 11/25
Curiosity, 10/3
Curriculum, 10/29
Custodial crew, 11/9
Daycare, 1/6
Decisions, 5/20
Deepening, 2/20
Desire, 12/26
Devotion, 9/25
Diligence, 10/11
Disabilities, 3/1
Discernment, 9/7
Discipleship, 9/30
Discipline, 9/16
Discussion, 2/9
Drama, 11/16
Eighth graders, 12/1
Elderly, 4/19
Empathy, 1/11
End of school year, 5/29
Endowment board, 4/4
Endowment fund, 10/12
English, 11/12
Enrollment, 9/1
Excellence, 9/8
Factions, 5/25
Faith, 1/4
Fall Enrollment, 5/30
Families, 1/20
Family churches, 4/16
Father, 2/11
Fathers, 4/23
Fear, 1/10
Fifth graders, 1/29
Finances, 12/8
Financial literacy, 5/9
First graders, 1/18
First responders, 2/24

Food service, 10/17
Foreign language, 11/11
Forgiveness, 12/17
Fourth graders, 1/28
Friendships, 10/19
Fundraisers, 5/2
Generosity, 9/22
Givers, 4/7
Giving, 4/8
Glory, 12/19
God's will, 12/11
Good Friday, 3/29
Goodness, 9/14
Government, 5/13
Grace, 1/9
Graduates, 2/13
Graduation, 2/23
Grandparents, 11/1
Gratitude, 10/1
Great commission, 4/30
Great-grandparent, 3/6
Grieving, 10/30
Growth, 9/26
Gymnasium, 10/22
Hallways, 10/24
Healing, 1/14, 12/29
Health, 2/12
Hearts, 12/23
Heaven, 5/19
History, 5/11
Holy Spirit, 9/29
Holy Week, 3/25
Homes, 10/20
Humility, 2/2
Identity, 3/21
Infant care, 2/4
Infants, 4/21
Influenza, 3/7
Insight, 3/19
Institutions, 11/30
Jesus Christ, 9/28
Joy, 9/19
Kingdom, 1/16
Leadership, 5/14
Learning, 2/29
Legacy, 12/3
Lent, 3/16

Library, 11/2
Life, 12/10
Light, 1/15
Listening, 2/1
Literature, 5/21
Local government, 1/8
Lord, 3/14
Lord's prayer, 5/4
Loss, 5/18
Lost, 4/18
Lunch period, 10/21
Marriages, 3/4
Math, 11/14
Maundy Thursday, 3/28
Mental health, 10/5
Mentors, 5/7
Mercy, 12/21
Middle school, 3/9
Military, 4/28
Minds, 4/6
Ministry, 4/2
Models, 5/6
Mothers, 4/22
Moving, 5/26
Music, 11/18
Nation, 4/29
Need, 1/13
Neighbors, 2/8
Next generation, 11/22
New blessings, 1/1
New families, 4/24
New year, 12/31
Obedience, 9/21
Office, 10/26
Order, 12/15
Parents, 3/3
Parking lot, 10/23
Partner schools, 2/28
Pastors, 2/21
Patience, 9/3
Perseverance, 12/28
Physical education, 11/6
Physical health, 10/8
Plans, 1/7
Playground, 10/25
Poise, 3/27
Police officers, 4/10

Potential, 5/3
Prayer, 1/24
Preparation, 3/18
Prepare for school, 9/2
Prepare the school, 9/3
Preschoolers, 1/17
Problem solving, 2/3
Process, 3/11
Professional development, 2/6
Protection, 1/2
Purity, 9/23
Purpose, 9/15
Reading, 4/11
Redemption, 12/25
Relationship, 3/20
Reorganization, 12/6
Repentance, 3/15
Reputation, 3/13
Respect, 10/15
Rest, 12/5
Resurrection, 3/22
Resurrection Day, 3/31
Retention, 10/9
Retired staff, 3/2
Return, 5/5
Reverence, 11/19
Righteousness, 1/12
Rule, 1/23
Safe travel, 10/31
Safety and security, 11/7
Salvation, 10/10
Schedules, 2/5
School leader, 12/13
School service, 5/10
Science, 11/15
Second graders, 1/26
Sensitivity, 9/12
Seventh graders, 12/2
Singing, 4/15
Sister schools, 3/12
Sixth graders, 12/9
Skill, 9/9
Social studies, 11/13
Space, 2/16

Speaking, 4/14
Special needs, 10/2
Spiritual struggles, 4/17
Sponsor churches, 1/22
Sports, 11/5
Starting school, 9/5
Stewardship, 3/10
Story, 1/21
Strangers, 5/15
Strength, 4/26
Striving, 9/18
Structure, 11/8
Struggles, 5/1
Student blessing, 5/22
Studies, 9/24
Summer break, 5/31
Support services, 12/7
Sustaining grace, 12/22
Teacher recovery, 5/28
Teachers, 11/10
Technology, 11/20
Thanks for year, 5/27
Third graders, 1/27
Time, 2/22
Transformation, 11/3
Tribes, 5/16
Truth, 9/13
Tuition, 9/20
Unborn, 4/20
Unity, 2/19
Vendors, 10/4
Victory, 11/27
Virtue, 10/13
Vocation, 2/14
Volunteers, 1/19
Wilderness, 4/1
Will, 3/8
Witness, 9/17
Wonders, 12/18
Word, 12/30
World, 4/27
Worldviews, 5/17
Worship, 11/24
Writing, 4/13

Prayer Guides

Address, 2/5
Attention, 12/3
Celebration, 1/18
Communion, 4/23
Concentration, 12/15
Confession, 2/2
Ease, 11/14
Elevation, 10/15
Gratitude, 1/9
Hearts, 9/20
Hierarchy, 3/18
History, 5/2
Home, 1/15
Honesty, 4/28
Humility, 2/17
Interest, 12/8
Intimacy, 10/29
Listening, 5/7
Liturgy, 9/26
Motives, 11/7
Place, 3/23
Posture, 4/4

Presence, 9/8
Primacy, 2/23
Priority, 3/10
Proximity, 1/2
Purity, 2/12
Reality, 2/28
Relationships, 12/25
Relevance, 11/21
Rest, 1/22
Revelation, 5/12
Savoring, 5/18
Secrecy, 1/27
Silence, 10/22
Simplicity, 11/26
Story, 4/9
Symphony, 5/22
Time, 3/4
Transformation, 10/1
Trust, 10/7
Unity, 4/15
Weakness, 3/30
Will, 9/15

Getting Started

You hear prayer warriors speak of *covering* people and their problems, and issues and their solutions, in prayer. You also hear how committed prayer from a body of believers has turned around whole families, whole neighborhoods, and even whole cities. If prayer even worked for the awful Nineveh, then it can work for us, no matter how far we have fallen or how much farther we must fall. Isn't that the good news of Jesus Christ?

When the Supreme Court banished government sanctioned prayer from public schools six decades ago, God wasn't listening. Or more to the point, God remained sovereign, and prayer remained every bit as effective. Indeed, prayer probably became more so in the darkness that fell over schools. People began to believe that no one could pray in any school when that error hadn't been the Supreme Court's ruling and may not have been its intent.

Whether you are a student, parent, or grandparent, or even a school principal, teacher, or volunteer, you may still pray for and in your public or private school. You may pray continually or, if not quite up to that feat, then often. You may certainly pray daily. You may coordinate your prayers with one, two, or three others, whether family members, friends, co-workers in the school, or school volunteers or neighbors. For when two or three gather in God's name, he comes running. Imagine what good could come if a whole school community prayed together daily.

You may already pray daily for your school and its students, families, leader, staff, and volunteers. That's a great start. Yet you may have found yourself repeating the same school prayer ad nauseam, day after day. Vain repetition, for the sound of the prayer rather than the thought behind it, is ineffective. God wants our hearts in prayer. Our tongues without love are only clanging cymbals. Noises do not attract his presence.

When your school prayers grow stale, let God work with what you've already asked, while you move on to other subjects. The subjects for school prayer are many because

our sins are many. But as many as our sins are, his mercy is far more plentiful. Ask with your head and heart. Persist as long as your head and heart remain in the prayer. But trust God with your prayer when you find your head or heart abandoning the subject, leaving your mouth running like an idling motor. As the following daily prayers show, the subjects for prayer are as plentiful as the days and even hours and minutes of the year.

Do our schools need prayer? Hah! Prayer is a struggle to invoke our God's sovereignty against powers and principalities that would otherwise rule and destroy us. For only in God's grace do we find our protection and redemption. So, where do you think those powers and principalities concentrate their efforts? Not in the clubs, bars, prisons, and other places where those dark powers rule. Pray for those places, too. But the point of God's spear, where he is ready to do his greatest work, is in the schools, where hope, promise, purpose, and a flourishing future dwell in students' hearts and souls.

You will find prayer guides and insights sprinkled throughout the 274 daily prayers in this book. Prayer is not just a habit, practice, discipline, and relationship. Prayer is also knowledge and skill. The prayer guides should remind you how fresh, deep, profound, purposeful, and effective prayer can be when pursued with the right motive and in the right relationship. May the prayer guides remind you of fruitful forms and powers of prayer. May they also help keep your prayers fresh and effective.

So, take up the following daily prayers for your school. Invite others to join you. Trust God. He delivers.

Daily School Prayers

September 1: Enrollment. Father God, you who rule the heavens and earth, who are sovereign, unrestricted, and wholly good, we ask today that you would confirm the school's enrollment in the hearts and minds of the school's families and their students. Give every parent the confidence in their choice of the school, that their student or students would learn, grow, and flourish throughout the year, meeting good friends, forming sound peer relationships, and receiving inspiring and effective instruction from teachers of your good character. Give every student the anticipation for a good year, as well as the will and discipline to make it so no matter what the year may present. Help the school's administrators finish enrollment details, welcoming new students and their families, while providing the information and encouragement they need for a good start to the school year. We ask these things in the name of our Lord and Savior Jesus Christ. Amen.

September 2: Preparing for School. Lord God, we love you and wish to bless you this new school year. Forgive us the sins of the summer as we prepare our hearts and minds, and prepare the hearts and minds of our students, for the new school year. Welcome the students and staff back into the school with your open arms, the arms that you so securely and graciously wrap around us to give us life and protect us from harm. Heal those who need healing to start the new year. Strengthen those who need your strength. Give courage to students who are anxious about the new school year. And above all, prepare the hearts and minds of the students to see you, learn of you, and embrace you through the school's teaching, learning, and activities throughout this new school year. We ask in the name of Jesus Christ. Amen.

September 3: Preparing the School. Dear Heavenly Father, we adore you, we worship you, and we give our day and lives to you, knowing that you will embrace us despite our fallen and broken state, because you love us and gave your Son for us. Walk with us through the day today, as we do our best to walk with you. We ask today, though, that you help the school's leaders, teachers, staff, and volunteers prepare the school's classrooms, common

areas, and grounds for the students of the school. Help us make the school shine, clean and orderly, ready to welcome the students in ways that give them hope and inspiration for a good school year. Let the floors gleam, the lawns be trimmed, and the hallway and classroom walls express the school's love for its students and for you. Help us ensure that the school is not only clean and orderly but also safe and secure, so that no student may suffer school injury or trauma this year. Open the hearts of the school leader, staff, and volunteers to welcome the students with joy and verve. We ask in Jesus' name. Amen.

September 4: Patience. Father God, maker of heaven and earth, you who judge and save and provide and befriend, we pray today that you would give every member of the school community your patience. As the teachers, students, administrators, and families rush to prepare for and begin the new school year, remind us to be patient with ourselves and others, and trusting with you. We know that you will bring to us what we need this year in the time we best receive it. Help the students to trust in you, that they learn by patient and enduring striving. Give the teachers your dose of mercy and grace, indeed of patience, with the students, and likewise give the students patience with their teachers as they learn what their teachers expect them to do. Make the school a community of trust and patient perseverance, so that the school may show the world the good you do in shaping the young for joyful service to you. We pray in the name of our Lord Jesus Christ. Amen.

September 5: Starting School. Our Father, who are in heaven. Today we hallow your name in the school. We wish your kingdom to come to the school and your will be done in the school, as your will is done in heaven. Give the school's students and staff your daily bread, and forgive the school's students and staff their sins, as they forgive those who sin against them. Do not lead the school's students to temptation but protect the students from the evil one. For thine is the kingdom and the power and the glory forever. Bless the school as it starts the new school year. Make the year one of fabulous growth and wondrous learning for every student of the school, a true blessing for every family of the school, and a rich ministry for every staff member of the school. Protect the school and lead the school. In Jesus' name we pray. Amen.

September 6: Construction. Heavenly Father, you who are our builder, our designer, and our provider of shelter and security and residence. The school undertook renovations over the summer, with your blessing and the means you provided through the hearts of benefactors of the school who gave generously to see the school grow. You brought to the school skilled and devoted workers. Now bring the work to completion so that the school may be orderly, attractive, safe, and clean. Energize the students and staff as they enter their new surroundings. And let the school's staff and leader put the newly renovated building to its proper use in pursuit of your mission for the school. Thank and reward the workers, on earth and in heaven. Thank and reward the donors, on earth and in heaven. And thank and reward the volunteers, too. In Jesus' name we pray. Amen.

September 7: Discernment. Father God, Almighty God of heaven and earth, you whom we revere and follow as our supreme sovereign, who rule the heavens and the earth with justice. We pray today that you would make the school community one of discernment, discerning above all your will and desire in all things.

Give us your ability to reason to exercise sound judgment in all things, from the students to the staff to the leadership of the school, that every member of the school community would have a sense and sensibility for your order, principle, and pattern in all things, from relationships to ministries to learning. We want to know your will and obey your word in all things. Make the students discerning in subjects, relationships, and self-control. Make the staff discerning in instruction, guidance, and discipline. Make the school leader and administration discerning in roles and responsibilities and accountability. Help us to know and follow your will. In Jesus' name we pray. Amen.

September 8: Excellence. Wonderful Counselor, Almighty God, you are a God of all excellence, of exquisite design and perfect rule. You err in nothing. Your judgments are divine. You have excellent knowledge, excellent character, and excellent grace. Share with us your excellence. Make the school community one that pursues and achieves excellence within your will. Help the students to excel in all things, from studies to relationships to generosity to your Spirit. Help the staff excel in instruction, learning, and inspiring the students to learn. Help the administration be excellent in organizing and guiding the school. Help the volunteers to show excellent service. Make the ministries and instruction of the school outstanding. We thank you for excelling in all things and helping us to do so as well. In Jesus' name we pray. Amen.

> **Presence.** Before you pray today, recognize God's presence with you. Wait until you sense that God is with you, alongside you, listening. As you begin to pray, remain aware of his hearing your prayer. Don't think about yourself and the words you are speaking, silently or aloud. Don't try to make your prayer articulate or fancy. Just think of God hearing your prayer as you speak it. Prayer is communication, even dialogue, with the living God. Prayer is not an incantation.

September 9: Skill. Heavenly Father, Prince of Peace, Supreme Sovereign, we stand in awe of your goodness and the goodness of your creation. You are a God of competence, of skill, with the finest of touches in all you do. You have made creation an example of your skill, your balance and design and consistency and proportion. You have made us capable of the finest skill. Make the school a ministry of skill, one where every student, staff member, and administrator shows competence in all things they do. Give the students the attention and concentration and devotion they need for skilled studies, writing, speaking, and the conduct of all things related to the school. Let skill be the hallmark of every action, whether in assignments, examinations, sports, music, drama, or other curricular, co-curricular, and extracurricular activities. Thank you for blessing us with capacity. Now help us to refine those capacities into practical application in skilled service to you. In Jesus' name we pray. Amen.

September 10: Compassion. Father God, you are a God of compassion. You care for the broken-hearted. You reach down to lift up the downtrodden. You care for the injured and the sick. Your heart goes out to the grieving. Make the school a place of your compassion. Help the students to show compassion for one another, reaching out to those whom they see are hurting or alone or struggling. Help the staff to teach compassion to the students and show compassion for the students and for one another. Let hearts go out for those who face loss, illness, injury, and challenges. Help us to grieve with those who grieve and mourn with those who mourn. Let us feel for one another so that all may feel loved in the way that you love. In Jesus' name we pray. Amen.

September 11: Care. Father of Glory, Father of Love, Father of Lights, we thank you for the care you show us in every need, how you heal us when we are broken, provide for us when we are poor, encourage us when we are down, and take interest in us in every moment. We are astounded at your care and concern, how you look to us when you have no need for us or from us. Your Son showed us your ultimate care in giving his life for us. Help the school to be a caring community. Help our students to care for one another, care for their parents and siblings and other family members, and care for their teachers and their school. Help the teachers instruct in care, guide in care, and model care so that the students may learn how to care. Help every member of the school community reach out when they see need, ask others how they are doing, and respond with the right words and actions to demonstrate care.

Teach us how you value us all and wish that we would all care for others as we care for ourselves. In Jesus' name. Amen.

September 12: Sensitivity. Loving Father, we adore you, we trust you, we desire you with all our hearts. You have shown us the sensitivity of your heart, the heart of your Son for the welfare and eternal salvation of all. You count the hairs on our head, you are so aware of our needs. Make the school a place of sensitivity, where every member

of the community is aware of the needs, interests, and ambitions of others, and respects those things. Make the school a place of sensitivity and interest and concern. Let no hard-heartedness linger among students or staff members. Help every student to show interest in others, growing beyond themselves. Help every staff member to see the needs and interests of students, and to provide for those things when appropriate. Make us aware of our neighbor's concerns and help us to act accordingly. We ask in Jesus' name. Amen.

September 13: Truth. Father God, God of destiny, God of life, and God of truth. We celebrate that you have spoken truth through your word, into our confused lives and communities. We thank you for the clarity of your truth, the confidence that we can have in it, and the order it brings to our lives. Make the school community a place where all share your truth, know your truth, seek your truth, and value your truth. Help the students to stand for truth, to recognize truth, and to distinguish your true word from the deceptions of the age. Help the school's staff members teach truth and model truth in their own lives for the students of the school. Guard the students against falsehoods and deceptions that would ruin their faith and destroy their lives. Help us to discern truth as a governing board and to celebrate your truth for the principles by which it organizes the school. In Jesus' name we pray. Amen.

September 14: Goodness. Heavenly Father, our Lord and Savior, we pray today for your goodness. We see the creation you made as good and as for our good, as we are to steward it according to your command and desires. We see you as the author of goodness against evil, setting an eternal standard of what is good against what constitutes evil. We attribute to you only good character and good actions, never bad, poor, or evil character, which is of the opposer, our adversary. Thank you for your goodness, the way that your creation shines with the rich life you have given it and the provider of life for us and your many other creations. Help the school to stand up for what is good, to see you as good, and to see good in your creation. Help the students to do good and to be good, and to avoid evil. Help the staff members instruct students in what is good and to guide the students into all goodness. In Jesus' name we pray. Amen.

September 15: Purpose. Dear Father, we pray today that you will give each student and staff member of the school a revelation of your purpose for their lives. We see you as a God of purpose, investing us with things to be and things to do that matter to you. You desire that we participate in your kingdom, that we give you glory, and that we do good in the world like you did good in the world through your Son, healing, feeding, serving, cleansing, rescuing, and instructing. Give us these good things to do as our purpose. Do not let us live aimless lives, selfish lives, or wasteful lives, but let every student of the school learn the purpose you have for them and then carry out that purpose diligently and creatively in their own lives, so that they may flourish under your sovereign rule and guidance. In Jesus' name we pray. Amen.

> **Will.** Your daily school prayer should always be that God's will, not our will, be done. Our prayers help us align our desires with his desires. As we pray, we are searching God's heart for his will for the school and for us. Your daily school prayer is shaping you to discern his will and desire that his will be done.

September 16: Discipline. Heavenly Father, you are a God of discipline. You discipline your children so that we prosper, not so that we suffer. Your word reminds us that a good father only disciplines his children, while those for whom he has no responsibility go undisciplined to their

peril. And so, make the school a place where your discipline is present, guiding, uplifting rather than oppressing, upholding your word and your desire that the students of the school receive your righteousness and live holy lives worthy of you. Help the staff and school leader to instill a sense of self-discipline in the students and then to discipline wisely, kindly, mercifully, and consistently to pursue the school's mission to shape hearts after you. Let every act of discipline be in the right time and right form and right measure, while guiding every student and parent to value discipline as for the good of the student and the school. We ask in Jesus' name. Amen.

September 17: Witness. Father God, your Son Jesus Christ was the light and a witness to the light. He points us to you as the light and the author of light. Make the school a witness to your glory. Help the students speak positively of you before others, so that others may witness your glory, too. Make the students beacons of your light. Let them tell others of your goodness. Help the school's staff members instruct the students how to witness to your truth and to the love of Jesus Christ. We are witnesses of your grand narrative, of your good news as the rescue from death. Let every member of the school community share the good news energetically and joyfully, to draw others to become their own witness to your glory. We pray in Jesus' name. Amen.

September 18: Striving. Father, Son, and Spirit, our glorious triune God, we pray today that the school would be a place of committed striving, where every member of the school community would seek diligently to do well for themselves and for others. We recognize that student effort, student striving, is a key to learning, that without effort students do not learn as they should. You have given the school the mission to educate their minds and shape their hearts, but the school cannot do so if the students do not put forth a good effort. Help the students of the school strive in their studies, strive in their physical education, strive in their sports, and strive in the formation of their own good character. Help the staff members create an atmosphere of healthy striving, recognizing and rewarding student effort. In Jesus' name we pray. Amen.

September 19: Joy. Holy Father, you whom we worship and adore, whom we celebrate as our provider and protector, and our rescuer from death. You have given the school community the good news of your Son's payment for our sins, in confession of which you have offered us eternal life. The students and staff members of the school accept your offer, celebrating their victory over death and their coming paradise with the joy that those future things deserve. Help make the school community a place of joy, of gladness and celebration over good things to come. Help the students to walk lightly and with confidence, happy even in their challenges because they know their victory in you. Make the school a place of gladness, where the smiles of all lift one another up, pointing anyone entering the school to you. In Jesus' name we pray. Amen.

September 20: Tuition. Heavenly Father, in whom we place our hope and trust, on whom we rely, and whom we celebrate, worship, obey, and adore. You have given the school the special trust of instructing the children of families in your word and how to serve you in your world. Families pay the school tuition for instructional services, without which the school would be unable to instruct as it does. Yet tuition is a heavy burden for many families. Our prayer today is that you would help make the school affordable to all families desiring to send their children to the school. Provide for each family the means of earning the income necessary to pay tuition, and help the school's staff and leadership find ways to reduce the burden of tuition. Make the school good stewards of tuition funds, and provide patrons, donors, benefactors, and family members to help needy families make tuition costs manageable. We thank you for keeping the school affordable and ask that you continue to do so. In Jesus' name we pray. Amen.

Hearts. When you sense God's presence, ready to listen to your prayer, move your heart into God's heart, and let God's heart fill your heart. Wait until your heart and God's heart are one, aligned. Begin your prayer only after you sense that your heart and God's heart are one.

September 21: Obedience. Father God, God of heaven and the earth, Supreme Sovereign, Ruler over All, we submit to your beneficent rule, to your commands, which we take to heart as for our own good. We are rebels by nature. Forgive our rebellion. Help us to see where we rebel, and help us to reflect complete obedience. Make the school a place where students obey the proper instructions and directives of their teachers and school staff and administrators. Help the students to quell their own

rebellion and instead to do as your word says and as the school's staff, administrators, teachers, and volunteers direct for the students' own good and safety. Make obedience a prime value in the school so that the school represents your hierarchy of delegated authority, your respect for those whom you have chosen to guide and instruct students in your way. Help teachers obey the school leader, and help parents obey school rules, norms, and customs, too. Make us obedient people, not hard of heart and hard of head but instead teachable. In Jesus' name we pray. Amen.

September 22: Generosity. Heavenly Father, Righteous Son, Holy Spirit, we adore and worship you, our triune God. You are the God of generosity, of favor, having chosen your adopted to enjoy all that you have. You have given your creation to your people, as the most extravagant of gifts. You bestow far greater favor on us than we'd ever deserve, having even given your own Son for us. Help the school to reflect your generous Spirit. Make the students of the school generous in the way that you are generous, with care and service to one another, for their families, and for their neighbors and friends. Help the staff of the school to model generosity toward the students and one another. And make the school generous toward the community. You are a God of extravagant gifts. Let the school reflect your generosity, even as we thank you for all that you give to the school and its students. In Jesus' name we pray. Amen.

September 23: Purity. Father God, we pray in your Spirit and out of your desire for our righteousness, that you would make us pure, that you would cleanse us with the blood of your Holy Son, and that we would reflect your own purity in all we are and do. Make the students of the school respect purity, value purity, and preserve and promote purity in their minds, their bodies, their pursuits, their relationships, and their ambitions. Do not let anyone pollute the spirits and souls of these innocent ones. Keep the students of the school innocent as doves, even if at the same time shrewd of the world's ways, so that the world does not deceive them out of their purity. For you are a Holy God and a righteous God, and we want to be pure of thoughts and actions, too, to honor you. In the name of Jesus, we pray. Amen.

September 24: Studies. Heavenly Father, we ask that you send your Spirit of insight, inspiration, striving, and discipline, to aid the students of the school in their studies, that you would make them skilled and knowledgeable. Help the school's students to be studious, interested in learning, and voracious in their appetites to know more about your world and especially more about you. Make scholars of the students, learners of the students, and teachers out of the students, too. Help the school's staff members to model good study habits, teach good study habits, and reward good study habits, too. We want the school's students to have minds for you and hearts for you, to serve you in your world. Bless the students of the school with your mind and heart for learning. In the name of Jesus, we pray. Amen.

September 25: Devotion. Father of all heaven and earth, glorious God, supreme Sovereign, we wish to devote our lives to you, knowing that as we do, you care for us, rescue us, comfort us, and provide for us. Commit the school to your devotion. Help the school's students learn what it means to devote themselves to you in all things. Help the school's staff teach students and model for students what devotion to you looks like. Make the school a community devoted to your heart, your service, and honoring you in all things. We devote the school, its students, its staff, its resources, and its graduates all to you because they are yours. In Jesus' name we pray. Amen.

September 26: Growth. Almighty God, you who knit each of us together in the womb, who creates all things and makes all things grow, we pray today that you would help the students of the school this school year to their fullest capacities. Help them grow physically, in stature and height and strength. Help them to grow mentally, in cognition and reason. Help them to grow socially, in responsibility and friendships. And above all, help them to grow spiritually, in knowledge of your loving character and in embrace of your salvation. Let the parents of the school's students see their children grow this year by leaps and bounds, in reading skill, in mathematics, social studies, science, history, English, Spanish, literature, and other academic subjects. Let the children grow in music, art, and dramatic skills. And just help them mature into godly young adults. In the name of Jesus, we pray. Amen.

Liturgy. Prayers can have a structure. We don't want to pray formulaically. God isn't a dispensary. But when we pray in the form of the Psalms or prophets, or after a long church tradition, we draw on powerful liturgical forms. Don't look for a formula. But don't discard liturgies.

September 27: Bible. Father God, you have given us your holy word. You have spoken through the prophets. Your people have carried your word through the millennia and into this generation. We treasure and revere your word, for you are the Word. Thank you for the Bible, for both its

Old and New Testaments, and for the grand narrative it gives us through which to know you and live out our lives. Help the students of the school love your word, keep it in their hearts, memorize it, and rely on it. Help the staff members of the school convey to the students their own love for your word and reliance on it. And bring the word from the school into the students' homes and communities, so that all may know your story, your good news, and your wisdom. In Jesus' name we pray. Amen.

September 28: Jesus Christ. Heavenly Father, you came into the world in the person of Jesus Christ our Lord, changing the course of history and giving us your good news. Your entry into your own creation astounds us. Your willingness to stoop so low as to give yourself for us shocks us to the core, changing our lives and outlooks entirely. We love you, Father, and we love and receive your Son Jesus Christ. Thank you for sharing your Son with the school. Place Jesus in the mind and heart of every student of the school. Give every student your presence, your encouragement, and your command. Let the teachers and other staff members of the school speak of Jesus, show the love of Jesus, and point every student toward Jesus. Make the school a place of his presence and his love and his excellence. In his own name we pray. Amen.

September 29: Holy Spirit. Almighty God, Father, Son, and Holy Spirit, thank you for your triune nature, for how you are not only Father to us and have not only offered your Son to us but how you also send your Holy Spirit to comfort, guide, and indwell us. Make the school a place where your Spirit walks and talks, and does your will, expressing your desires to the school's students and staff. Let us carry your Spirit richly and consistently. And help the students and staff and volunteers to share your Spirit, to welcome your Spirit, and to celebrate your Spirit as we celebrate you the Father and your Son Jesus Christ. Let your Spirit share your counsel liberally, alerting students to their needs for confession and repentance. Let your Spirit be their guide and conscience. And help students to carry your Spirit into their homes. In Jesus' name we pray. Amen.

September 30: Discipleship. Father God, your Son Jesus Christ made disciples out of fishermen, and so he can make disciples out of us. Help the students of the school be disciples of Jesus Christ, not just knowing Jesus but also following Jesus to study his words and person, to emulate him, and to carry him into their world to share with others. Let the model and teachings of Jesus Christ sink deeply into every student's mind, conscience, and spirit, so that they become Christ-like. Let their parents see how they change because of their instruction at the school in the discipleship of Jesus Christ. Don't just let students learn the ways of the world at school. Let them learn your ways and follow your ways, as you walk with them and in them through their lives and communities as you once walked with the disciples. And let the teachers, administrators, and volunteers at the school model discipleship in Jesus Christ. Help us all to be disciples of Jesus Christ. In his name we pray. Amen.

October 1: Gratitude. Dear Father, we are so thankful for your blessings, your good news, your gift, your presence, and your provision. Make the school a place of gratitude. Fill the hearts of students with thankfulness, with appreciation for all you do for them and for their families and the school. Help the students to see your work in everything they receive and do. Help them to know that you are the author of their very lives. Give them the deepest gratitude for you, your Son Jesus Christ, and your Holy Spirit. Help them to see how gratitude should rule their inner lives so that they draw close to you and rely on you and honor you. Let the teachers and other staff members and volunteers reflect and teach gratitude for the students to learn and emulate. We thank you for the school, and we ask that you give us more gratitude. In Jesus' name we pray. Amen.

> **Transformation.** Your words form you. The words you think and express shape your desires, actions, and identity. God's declaration that his Son is the Word indicates the power that words have over us and our actions and identity. Your school prayer, aligning with his will, is thus transforming you, even as it benefits the school and its students.

October 2: Special Needs. Heavenly Father, you have blessed the school with students who have special needs. We thank you for them. We see in them your creation, your love, your own image, just as we see those attributes in others. Help the school community to lift up students who have special needs, to satisfy those needs, and to encourage the students to develop their capacities to the full. Help the teachers of the school to recognize how best to serve students who have special needs, and help the school to equip those teachers. Let the school's treatment of special needs students reflect your love, service, and desire to see them reach their potential to serve you. Help us to treat them respectfully without diminishing their worth and value to you and the school. In Jesus' name we pray. Amen.

October 3: Curiosity. Father God, you have made us curious beings. You have given us imaginations and interests and ambitions that lead us forward. We thank you for making us interested in the world, curious about how the world works, and concerned about others. Make the school a place of curiosity especially about you, your Son Jesus Christ, and your role in creation. Help the students to express the right curiosity about the right subjects, like righteousness and holiness and your word. Help the teachers and other staff members and volunteers to express curiosity and wonder, and inspire students to do the same. Make the students in awe of your creation and your work in creation, especially your work in them. And satisfy students' curiosity with a revelation of your work and wonders, so that they continue lifelong to pursue you. In Jesus' name we pray. Amen.

October 4: Vendors. Almighty God, thank you for all you provide for the operation of the school in its pursuit of your mission for it, to educate minds and shape hearts in service to you. Thank you for the individuals and businesses providing supplies and materials for the school's students and staff, for the building and grounds. Thank you for their skill, their competence, their devotion, and the generosity they show in sharing their goods and services with the school. We ask that you bless them for doing so, for supporting your ministry. Reward them here and in heaven. Provide for them in their businesses and in their homes. Protect them and their families, and above all, bring them closer to you and to their salvation under the blood of your Son Jesus Christ. In Jesus' name we pray. Amen.

October 5: Mental Health. Lord God, who gives us our very minds, our reason, the ability to live in your creation with a consciousness of you and your glory and the salvation you have for us. We know the challenges that the students of the school face in their mental health, the anxiousness of the world that oppresses them, the depressions and disabilities that affect their minds, souls, and spirits. We ask that you guard them against these

attacks on their cognition and consciousness, their balance and sense of being near to you, their ability to complete their studies to learn more of you and your creation. We ask that you heal their minds and spirits, that you restore their good mental health, that you give them the concentration and attention and mental resources to continue to learn about you, learn about themselves, and live flourishing lives in witness to your good news. Encourage the staff with the skills to recognize mental health issues among the students, and bless the school with the mental health resources and professionals to help the students. Do likewise for the staff members and their families. We need you. In Jesus' name we pray. Amen.

October 6: Collaborative Schools. Father God, Heavenly Father, Prince of Peace, we pray today for the schools sharing with our school in collaboration. Bless their ministries of Christian education. Teach their students about you. Protect the students and staff of those schools, and raise them up as a light in the region attracting others to you. Grow their enrollment and bless their finances. Encourage their staff members and leaders. Continue to educate the children of the region through collaborative schools so that more of our next generation know your love for them and share the good news. Enrich the ministries of those schools, as you do for the school. We love you, Lord. In Jesus' name we pray. Amen.

October 7: Community. Almighty God, our Lord and Savior, we pray today for the surrounding community around the school and the homes of the families of the school students. We pray that all in those communities would know you and receive your salvation. We ask that you secure the community, keep it safe, keep its residents strong and healthy and hopeful for your eternal paradise, as you offer us that hope, too. We ask that the community surrounding the school support and respect and value the school. Let the community surrounding the school know that the school stands for you and, in doing so, stands for them, too. Help the school's students and staff members to know the needs of the community and to serve those needs in witness of your love. In Jesus' name we pray. Amen.

Trust. As you conclude your prayer today, trust that God will answer it. Jesus exhorts that we should believe when we pray, so that his Father may do as we ask. Believing when praying means trusting that God will do as we ask, or indeed, do more and better than we ask. Do not pray disbelieving or doubting. Doubt and disbelief do not exhibit faith. Faith is an essential ingredient in effective prayer, in the way that Jesus exhorts it.

October 8: Physical Health. Father God, you who are our maker, our creator, our provider, and the author of our lives. The students of the school need you for their physical health, physical safety, and physical growth. It is so hard to be young but ill, weak, injured, or disabled. Protect the students against physical hardship, physical trauma, injury, and disability. Heal their physical issues, heal their bodies as well as their spirits and souls. Make them strong. Help the school to give them physical exercise and nutrition and attention to make their physical selves healthy and active and strong, to pursue your ministry for them as witnesses to your love. We ask these things in Jesus' name. Amen.

October 9: Retention. Heavenly Father, thank you for blessing the school with skilled and dedicated teachers and other staff members. You have given them your gift of excellence, of devotion to the upbringing of the young in the way that Jesus said to let the little children come to him. Thank you for bringing these staff members to the school with the heart to instruct the school's students in your word and in the beauty and design of your creation. We pray today that you help the school retain its skilled and dedicated staff members, compensating them fairly, encouraging them in their development, and showing them the care and support they deserve as your gifts to the school. Help the school to sustain their morale and encourage their loyalty. Let the staff members carry out their ministries at the school in ways that encourage them that they are storing up treasures in heaven. In Jesus' name we pray. Amen.

October 10: Salvation. Almighty God, you who are our rescuer from the death brought upon us by our disobedience and the fall of humankind in your good world. You have brought salvation to us through the life, death, and resurrection of your Son Jesus Christ in whom we trust. We pray today that all students of the school would know Jesus as their Lord and Savior, would confess their sins, repent of their sins, and trust in his resurrection that they, too, may have eternal life. Let every student receive salvation. Secure the students in eternal life, from their first day at the school to their last day on earth. Let them enter your kingdom and receive their inheritance. Let them see and enjoy your paradise. We pray the same for their family members and for every staff member, volunteer, and guest who enters the school. In Jesus' name. Amen.

October 11: Diligence. Father God, you have blessed the school with a ministry to your children, the students whom believing and trusting families send to the school to educate their minds and shape their hearts for service to you in your creation. Help the school's staff members and volunteers to instill in the students a spirit of diligence, that every student would treat the privilege of Christian education with its due, and that every student would attend

to the responsibilities given to them in their studies. Make the students of this school so diligent in their studies and in their lives that your light shines through them. Help them to know what their teachers require of them and to address those things promptly without procrastination. Help students of the school become responsible for their own learning and faith rather than having others be responsible for them. Make the students diligent, and help the staff demonstrate and model diligence for the students in ways that inspire the students to act, serve, and succeed. In Jesus' name we pray. Amen.

October 12: Endowment Fund. Father God, you have blessed the school with an endowment fund that provides substantial scholarship relief for the students of the school. Help the endowment fund to grow so that more students can attend at lower cost to their needful parents, so that your word may grow in the hearts of the community's children. Bring more donors to the point of giving more funds to the endowment fund so that the endowment fund may bless this generation and future generations. Secure the endowment fund against loss. Help the endowment fund board discern the best investments to make to see the fund grow to accomplish its purpose in pursuit of the school's mission to have students learn to serve you. In Jesus' name we pray. Amen.

October 13: Virtue. Father God, you are a virtuous God, one who is holy, above all things, set apart from the corruption of humankind and of the world. Make the school a community that loves virtue, values virtue, teaches virtue, and rewards virtue, as a character after your own heart. Your Son Jesus Christ was the model and paragon of virtue, flawless and perfect in every word and action. Help the students model their lives on Jesus, pursuing his perfection as their own, discerning the thoughts, words, attitudes, and actions Jesus reflected and his Spirit as our conscience recommends to us. Help the staff members teach virtue and recognize and reward virtue among the students. In Jesus' name we pray. Amen.

October 14: Boys and Girls. Our Father, who made each of us in your image, and who also made us male and female. We acknowledge our brokenness, even in understanding who we are as your creations. We see our confusion and the confusion of others when we don't want to be confused. Growing up is such a time of transition, of learning how to behave as a child, youth, and adult, both with respect to ourselves and in respect of others. Help the boys and girls of the school accept your identity for each of them, in your Son Jesus Christ. Keep boys respectful of boys and girls, and girls respectful of girls and boys, both in their similar capacities, interests, and ambitions, and in their different capacities, interests, and ambitions. In Jesus' name we pray. Amen.

October 15: Respect. Heavenly Father, you who deserve our utter respect, you whom we revere, we pray today that students of the school would likewise respect and revere you, while also learning to respect one another as created in your image. Help the students of the school to follow your Golden Rule of treating others as they would have others treat them. Help the students of the school treat their differences with others as things to acknowledge and respect, while not holding one another apart. Rid the students of all bias and prejudice, while keeping them discerning of the sources of those faults. Help students not to offend and insult one another, while also helping them to forgive one another for offenses and insults. Keep the peace of the school, while allowing students to express and celebrate their differences. Make respect reign in the school as it does in heaven. In Jesus' name we pray. Amen.

October 16: Board Members. Almighty God, you who are our supreme sovereign, our leader, our governor, and our ruler, we pray today for the board members of the school, not only for their discernment and wisdom but for each of them personally and in their families. Keep the board members strong and healthy. Provide the income and other means for them to maintain their homes and provide for their families while also being generous with the school. Keep the board members committed to the school's flourishing, conscious of its mission, and joyful in their service. Protect each board member against accident and illness, against allegation and misfortune and strife. Comfort board members needing consolation, heal board members needing physical recovery, and share your peace with board members needing encouragement. Let every board member participate appropriately, sharing their own experiences, skills, and insights, in unity and with respect for others. We pray in Jesus' name. Amen.

> **Elevation.** Your daily school prayers are not putting coins in a vending machine to receive what it offers. The words you express in prayer elevate the highest in the heart of God, preparing you and the ones for whom you pray to receive what God offers. You are not imposing your will on reality. Your words reach up into heaven to participate in what heaven will soon accordingly offer.

October 17: Food Service. Father God, you who feed us with your word, your bread from heaven, while also providing for us in your creation out of the goodness of your generosity and the rich harvest you bring. Thank you for the staff members and volunteers who work in the school's food service, providing nutritious meals for the school's students. Help them to prepare nourishing food, safe food, and delicious food for the students to enjoy. Help the parents pay for the food without hardship. And help the students respect the efforts and ministry of the food service workers and volunteers. Protect those workers and volunteers, reward them here on earth and in heaven, and continue to guard and protect their families. Encourage them in their service, and bring more skilled food service workers and volunteers to the school in times of need. In Jesus' name we pray. Amen.

October 18: Classroom Aides. Heavenly Father, you are our aid, our provider, rescuer, guide, and comforter. You have blessed the school with skilled, devoted, and sensitive classroom aides. Hearten them in their ministry. Encourage them in their devotion and skills. Help the students and parents and staff let the classroom aides know we respect and value them in their service to the students of the school. Let their words be your words of kindness and humility and instruction and discipline. Help them to ease the pains, quell the fears, and stop the tears of the students, and to turn the students to their lessons to learn more about you and your creation. Reward and protect the school's devoted aides, and bring to the school more who share their skill and devotion. Heal them when they need healing, provide for them, and equip them for their ministry, while also protecting and providing for their family members. In Jesus' name we pray. Amen.

October 19: Friendships. Our Father, you sent your Son Jesus Christ to be not only our Savior but also our brother and even our friend. We see in the friendships within the school the evidence of your presence, the work of your Spirit. Bless and encourage those friendships. Help the school's students learn to care for one another in their friendships, to guide one another, and to forgive one

another. Multiply the friendships among students, both students with similar backgrounds and interests and students whose backgrounds and interests are far apart. Make lasting friendships that extend over the summers, into high school, and beyond, even into a lifetime. Let the friendships flourish not only in the school but on the playground and outside of school. And let the friendships honor you in every way, in holiness, righteousness, and purity. In Jesus' name we pray. Amen.

October 20: Homes. Father God, you are our shelter. You make a room for us in your heavenly home, which will soon be our home. But until we join you in paradise, we reside here in your creation, in our own homes. Make the homes of the students of the school places of safety and security, not of strife. Keep the homes of the students stable and fit for the raising of your young. Help the parents of the students of the school to make the rent, mortgage, and tax payments on their residences, to keep their homes in good sanitation, maintenance, and repair, and to bring your word and Spirit into their homes so that the school's students may know you and grow closer to you and obey you through their knowledge of Jesus Christ your glorious Son. Dwell richly in the homes of the school's students. In Jesus' name. Amen.

October 21: Lunch period. Wonderful Counselor, King of kings, we thank you for the nourishment of the bodies of the students of the school at lunch period. We thank you for the rest and recovery and fellowship and friendship the students find at the lunch period, for the joyful noise they raise. Help the staff and volunteers make the lunch period a time of peace and order, even as it is also a time of nourishment and play. Guard the students against dispute, and help them to show kindness and generosity to one another. Let even the lunch period of the school honor you. In Jesus' name we pray. Amen.

October 22: Gymnasium. Almighty God, you who live in glorious splendor, on high, in your eternal home, before your court, and as supreme sovereign over all. We wonder at your willingness to stoop so low as to regard us as your image and to care for our needs. We do not deserve your consideration but accept it as our greatest possible gift, though we know we have offended you in disobedience of your commands and desires and disregard of your great gift. We thank you for the large and bright gymnasium you have shared with the school community, for instruction in physical exercise and for sports and other play throughout the day, evening, and weekend. We thank you for gifting the staff of the school with the creative and inspirational use of the gymnasium, for physical training, drama, worship, community, and school celebrations, and in so many other ways. Let the play and instruction and worship in the gymnasium please you, in kindness and fair competition and fun activity and wholehearted enjoyment of you. In Jesus' name. Amen.

> **Silence.** God's answer to your prayer may be silence. We should not despair when we sense that God's response isn't encouraging affirmation or even prompt action but instead simply silence. If, after you pray, you get the strong sense that God's response is only silence, then trust that in God's silence he is already doing the work that the right answer to your prayer demands. His silence may be working on your heart, faith, and trust. His silence may accomplish exactly what you need and ask.

October 23: Parking Lot. Heavenly Father, you who are our Lord and Savior, our Provider and Counselor, our Prince of Peace. We revere you, giving you praise, today and every day. We thank you for blessing the school with a large parking lot for the school's use. Help the school community keep the parking lot a place of order and safety, that every drop off and pick up would go smoothly and without injury, and that every user of the parking lot would do so sensitively and kindly, with thanks to the church and respect for its membership and staff. Help the school to maintain the parking lot appropriately, using it as a proper resource for pursuit of your glorious mission for the school, that every child would have a mind and heart for you, to serve you in your creation. In Jesus' name we pray. Amen.

October 24: Hallways. Dear Father, you who taught your disciples to teach, to move about the countryside, to reach those who need to hear your word, we pray today for the peace, order, and respect in the hallways of the school, as students move about to learn more of your world. Let the hallways be places of order and of joy, of rest from instruction and of recovery, and of greeting and kindness, where friendships blossom, and students meet and greet kindly others whom they don't know. Let hugs and high fives and smiles be the order of the hallway. Quell fights and disputes. Stop shoving and harsh words. Let locker mates be kind to one another. Help students to help one another in the hallways. And let the hallways be clean and attractive, too, with students contributing to the care of the school. Let everyone who enters the school's hallways feel the love of Jesus Christ our Lord. We pray in his name. Amen.

October 25: Playground. Our Father, you who are not only a God of law and rule and creation but also of love and care and even play. We remember how your Son Jesus Christ let the children come to him, and we want the same for the students of the school, that they would joyfully run to him. Help the teachers and aides and volunteers to guide the students on the playground in a proper spirit of play and fun and physical exercise, in kindness and gentleness to one another, with respect for the physical and mental health of one another, without strife or carelessness or harsh words. Let the students learn to play with one another without faction and cliques. Help the students to welcome all students into their play. Silence mean words,

while giving the students a gentle and kind voice for the needs and interests of one another. Help the students to share playground equipment generously, taking turns. In Jesus' name we pray. Amen.

October 26: Office. Father God, you who are our administrator and our chief executive, who guides us in all wisdom and judgment, we honor you and seek to follow you as the leader of the school. We pray today for the office staff, that the receptionist and directors and leaders remain strong, stable, and healthy, devoted to the students of the school and the school's mission, skilled in leadership and organization and administration, discerning in judgment, and sensitive to the needs of the students, families, staff, and school community. Give them strength, good health, rest, restoration, vision, and all the other characteristics they need to do well for you, in service to you, after your heart, as models and guides for all who enter the school. Keep your Spirit in the office, for student comfort, healing, accountability, discipline, and encouragement. Keep your Spirit of joy in the office, to bless all who enter. And keep your Spirit of love for the good news of Jesus Christ, that all who enter would know him and receive his salvation. In Jesus' name. Amen.

October 27: Architects. Heavenly Father, you have brought to the school talented and skilled and devoted architects and planners who have the insight and inspiration to plan and design a suitable building expansion to meet current and future enrollment needs. Bless and guide that team of architects. Help them shape suitable plans that both meet the school's needs and provide a light, stimulating, proportional, efficient, safe, secure, and beautiful new addition to the school. Keep the architectural team healthy, informed, unified, and inspired. Let their designs honor you and represent you in their beauty, proportion, and functionality. And draw the architects to you, if they do not know you, and if they do know you, then let them be a witness to you and perform in your service. Bless also their architectural ministry and their families and churches. In the name of Jesus, we pray. Amen.

October 28: Building Fund. Father, Son, and Spirit, you have increased the enrollment of the school so substantially that the school has run out of classrooms. Its gymnasium cannot hold all its students. The school has been good stewards, finding additional classrooms within its current walls, but still the school needs more classrooms. You have placed plans for expanding the building on the hearts and minds of the school's staff, leader, and board. But the school doesn't have the funds to build according to plans yet. You pour out blessings. You open the storehouses. You open the hearts of the donors. We honor you and devote to you every resource you provide toward the building fund. We thank you for blessing the building fund, for enabling the school to build according to its needs, to do as you will in the instruction of more students in your word and way. In Jesus' name we pray. Amen.

October 29: Curriculum. Father God, you have blessed humankind with your word and your capability to reason. You have further given the school a ministry of instruction in your word and in the many subjects that help us understand and prosper in your creation. These subjects make up a complex and overlapping mix, one that we call a curriculum. Help the school's leader and teachers and administrators to design and maintain a curriculum that truly brings to life your word and the students' ability to learn and reason, as well as to acquire the knowledge and skills to serve you in your wondrous creation. Strengthen the curriculum where it is weak, correct the curriculum where it is wrong, remove the overlaps, fill the gaps, and help the teachers and support staff to understand their role in teaching the curriculum. Guide and strengthen the school's curriculum director. Make the curriculum yours, after your heart, in pursuit of your will, to train up and instruct this next generation of your children. In Jesus' name we pray. Amen.

> **Intimacy.** Your daily school prayer is to your heavenly Father. You thus pray with a sort of intimacy, like a child speaking to its mother or father. Pray with the openness, need, closeness, and confidence of a child speaking to the most loving and generous parent.

October 30: Grieving. God of Compassion, God of Sorrows, the school has suffered losses, deaths of students and staff members and family members of staff members and students, also of graduates and family members of graduates. We are a people of sorrow in those times, but we also rejoice in those times knowing that our believing family members and friends are simply returning home to you, joining you in your paradise kingdom, in your embrace, with your rescue even from death. We miss those departed but saved souls, and we struggle not knowing when we will see them again. Comfort those of us who grieve, who have suffered such loss, or who anticipate such loss soon. You are our God of comfort and God of grief, weeping with those of us who weep, and mourning with those of us who mourn. Give us the strong assurance of the salvation of the departed and departing, and help us to witness to your good news often and richly to those not yet departed and not yet secure in your salvation. We ask these things in Jesus' name. Amen.

October 31: Safe Travel. Father, Son, and Spirit, we pray that you would travel with the commuting students and parents of the school, protecting them on the highways, bringing them safely to school and returning them safely home. Keep them from harm's way on the highways, and keep their transportation working properly so that the  students of the school may attend timely and regularly, while also returning home timely to rest, study, and return to the school. Also protect the travel of the school's students, parents, and teachers to distant locations, whether by bus or car on field trips or by plane and other means of travel on foreign missions. Help finance the travel, secure the travel, and conduct the transportation timely and safely to distant destinations and back home. We ask in Jesus' name. Amen.

November 1: Grandparents. Father God, we thank you for the generations you have taught at the school. We thank you for the generations standing behind the current students of the school. We thank you not only for the parents but also for the grandparents who are such a steady blessing to the school. Bless the grandparents of the school for their devotion to you and their commitment to the school's mission. Bless their grandchildren. Give the grandparents ministries of prayer, financial giving, and volunteering, also mentoring and training and educating students of the school. Thank you for every grandparent. We pray that you would heal them, bless them, protect them, and provide for them, as they do for us, the school, and you. Let us also give the school's grandparents the honor, recognition, care, and time they are due. In Jesus' name we pray. Amen.

November 2: Library. Lord God, thank you for the blessing of your good book, the Bible, both under the Old Covenant and under the New Covenant in the blood of your Son Jesus Christ. We are a people of the book, your good book. We thank you for making us a people of your good book, a people of your word. We put your word at the center of our lives, reading your good book daily and taking to heart its lessons brought to us by your Spirit. Fill the library of the school with books that point to your good book and your good news, the gospel of Jesus Christ. Help the school's students open your good book and learn from other books in the library about your story, the gospel or good news. Bless the library ministry, as it points students to you. Help the librarian and teachers of the school make good use of the library's resources to pursue the school's mission after you. In Jesus' name. Amen.

November 3: Transformation. Lord Jesus Christ, you who transform the mind, body, and soul, in resurrection with you, we ask that you help the teachers of the school to teach for that very transformation, that the students of the school would receive your Holy Spirit, would find new life in you, and would shine the light of their transformation into the school, their classmates, their family members at home, and their community. Help the teachers understand the goal, purpose, and efficacy of teaching for transformation, whether shared programmatically or simply through your Spirit. Let the students of the school receive instruction in a transformative manner, not simply to add knowledge to a secular soul but to receive your regeneration in Christ, with a new body and spirit and soul. In Jesus' name we pray. Amen.

November 4: Committees. Heavenly Father, you are the Holy One who gathers your chosen in community, to work together toward all good things. You have blessed the school with committees made up of parents, staff, and volunteers to facilitate the education of students in your way according to your word. Help the leader, board, and staff of the school to find the right committee members, and help the committee members organize and work for the benefit of the students of the school. Find the right mission for the committees and promote the right committee relationships to advance your will. Let the work of the school's committees bless the students, families, and school. In the name of Jesus, we pray. Amen.

November 5: Sports. Father God, you are the one who stimulates the body and mind to compete, to meet challenges, and to strive. We thank you for the sports programs and facilities of the school. We thank you for the dedicated parents, volunteers, and staff supporting the school's sports teams and programs. We thank you for the public and community facilities where the school's teams play. We thank you for the referees and umpires who enforce the rules and customs of the sport. We ask that you help each student participate in sports in your good Spirit, with fair play, and without injury. We ask for your continued blessing on the school's sports program and that you would develop each student to their full capacity to participate joyfully in sports. In Jesus' name we pray. Amen.

November 6: Physical Education. Heavenly Father, you who make the strong and equip the skilled, and develop the persevering, and reward the committed and disciplined, we

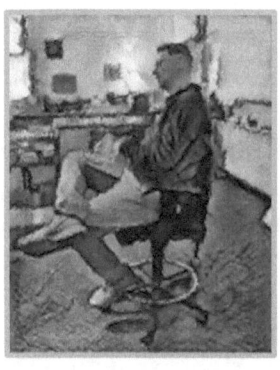

thank you for blessing the school with a gifted physical education teacher, a special physical education program, and a fine gymnasium, equipment, and playground. We thank you for helping the students to exercise safely and often, for their good health and strength. Develop the bones, muscles, and other physiology of the students to participate vigorously in physical education. And give the physical education instructor the stamina, insight, and creativity to make physical exercise a constant joy. In Jesus' name we pray. Amen.

Motives. As you pray, examine your heart and listen to your words to ensure you pray with the right motives. God's word says he does not answer our prayers when we pray with the wrong motives. God's word includes as wrong motives, to spend on our pleasures what God grants us. Instead, pray to get hold of God more so than to receive God's answers. Seek God's kingdom first, and then he'll grant the things we ask.

November 7: Safety and Security. Dear God, you are our protector, sheltering us under your wing from all harm. You are the one who keeps us from the adversary, who disarms the strong, who alerts the believers to coming harm, who equips the police with the skills and dedication to protect the school. Keep us at our posts, watching for harm and preventing harm. Keep the school safe and its property secure. Deter the vandal and the violent. Bring peace to relationships of strife, and unmask and expose the attacker. Keep the students of the school from all harm, and secure the school's furnishings and resources against theft. Do not let the embezzler touch the school's finances, nor the thief to steal the school's equipment. Thank you for keeping the school and its students and staff safe from all attacks. In Jesus' name we pray. Amen.

November 8: Structure. Father, Son, and Spirit, Holy God, three in one, you order and structure all things within your hierarchy of values, everything having its place, higher or lower, and everything having its relationship, while everything also having its value. The school has grown larger in its enrollment and thus has grown more complex in its programs and administration. Help the school leader and board find the right structure to administer the school wisely, as you would have the school leader do. Reveal the structure that will provide the most value, order, clarity, and confidence for the school to carry out its mission most effectively, to educate student minds and shape student hearts for service to you. Reveal your designs in the school's administration. And then help the school leader carry out those designs with the confidence of the staff, students, families, and board. In Jesus' name. Amen.

November 9: Custodial Crew. Almighty God, you have given the school a clean, new, fresh, orderly building and grounds, maintained with great effort by a custodial crew. The crew works hard, may receive little pay for all they do, and may suffer health issues, too, leading to turnover in the custodial staff. We ask that you protect, heal, and reward the custodial staff for all they do for the school and for you. Help them keep the school clean and in good order. Protect them against all manner of harm. Strengthen them for the important ministry they do. And give the school's teachers and leaders and volunteers a heart for the custodial staff, to respect them and value all they do. In Jesus' name. Amen.

November 10: Teachers. Heavenly Father, you who created each one of us in your image, we thank you for bringing such gifted teachers to the school and uniting them after the mission to educate student minds and shape student hearts for service to you. Thank you for giving the school's teachers the hearts for students and the minds for teaching and learning. Thank you for keeping them safe and healthy, for inspiring them to bring new ways of learning, and for dedicating their ministries to the students of the school. Heal the teachers who need healing, encourage the teachers who need encouragement, and guide the teachers who need guidance, in the gentle and humble way you do. Keep the school's teachers healthy, keep them loving you, and help them to teach the students your word in all they do. Bring more talented teachers to the school, and develop the skills of the teachers who are here already, so that they help the school become a leader in preparing students for high school, college, and great marriages, families, and careers. And reward the teachers of the school, both here and in heaven where rewards are greater. In Jesus' name. Amen.

November 11: Foreign Language. Holy Father, thank you for the love of other languages and cultures that you have instilled in the school community, for you are a lover of all. You are the creator and sustainer of culture and the author of reason and the word. Thank you for the foreign-language and language-immersion programs at the school, for the skilled and dedicated teachers you have brought to the program, the families who want their children to learn a foreign language, and the students who embrace language as a bridge to other cultures and peoples. Make the teachers strong and the students curious and striving learners of the language. Lead the students in an interest in the culture, and when the students travel to foreign-language-speaking lands, give them an openness for the people and an understanding of their language and ways. In Jesus' name. Amen.

November 12: English. Father God, you have given us the gift of language, not to build kingdoms of our own in the air, Towers of Babel, but through which to know and obey you. You have given us your word, which we have translated into our own English language so that we may read your word to understand and obey it. Help the teachers

of the school inspire students to acquire English language skills like spelling and grammar, so that they may be skilled readers and writers, with the communication skills to become preachers, pastors, ministers of your word, and business leaders, government leaders, and leaders of charitable organizations. Give the English teachers the strength and consistency and insight and sensitivity to inspire and guide students, so that the school becomes a leader in teaching English. In Jesus' name. Amen.

November 13: Social Studies. God Almighty, you are the God of relationship, fellowship, brotherly and sisterly love, and intimacy. You are the one who forms and authorizes and structures society. Help the social studies teachers of the school teach the subject soundly, with your word and commands in mind, so that students of the school may acquire the knowledge of how you structure society and its relations. Give the students of the school a heart for how your word operates in society, to structure social relations.

And let them acquire a righteous character through which to govern their social relations with others, starting in the family, among their friends and classmates in the school, in their churches, and in the community. Strengthen the social studies teachers and programs of the school. Let the school be a leader in social studies. In the name of Jesus. Amen.

November 14: Math. Dear Father, you are the God of counting and measurement. You count the hairs on our head. Your word is filled with numbers from the triune godhead and Christ's three days in the tomb to the seven days of creation to the twelve tribes and disciplines to the forty days of fasting in the wilderness. Help the students of the school to love numbers, in your word and in your world, as a tool for knowing you and seeing your design. Help the students see how numbers can make a difference in their own lives, as they learn to budget, measure, and count, and enter careers like accounting, banking, financial advising, engineering, and the sciences that depend on numbers. Give the math teachers of the school the sensibility, materials, and inspiration to encourage students in learning math skills. Make the school a leader among schools in teaching math to its students, so that they may graduate with skills to serve you. In Jesus' name. Amen.

> **Ease.** Your daily school prayer to your Father should come with the ease with which a child speaks to its parent. Don't hesitate to approach God's throne in prayer if you come with the right motive. Pray with the ease with which you would ask something that the most loving parent would already want to give a wholly deserving child. Jesus paid that price to open his Father's heart to your prayer.

November 15: Science. Father God, the God of reason, the God of the word, the God of design, thank you for giving us the rationality and insight of your word. Thank you for forming the foundation of science in your reason, principle, and pattern. Thank you for creation that submits to rational investigation, for a world that follows perceptible laws. Thank you, too, for giving us science to improve our lives, in which to establish medicine, engineering, economics, materials science, psychiatry, and so many other professional fields. We commit the science classes and teaching and programs of the school to you. Guide the science teachers of the school to communicate the ethical bounds of science in your word and the rational nature of science in your word and law. Help the students of the school see science as not only compatible with your word but as grounded in your word. Let the students acquire a deep knowledge of science in which they see careers in the science fields as ministries serving you. In Jesus' name. Amen.

November 16: Drama. Heavenly Father, you have given us your grand narrative, your great drama, your unparalleled story, and you have made us a part of your story. We thank you for that story and for the good news that we are yours, in your great drama, as your history unfolds. Help the students of the school see the dramas in which they participate, the plays that they put on for the school, as reflecting your grand story. Make the dramas of the school be to your credit and glory. Give the staff members and volunteers who guide the students in dramatic skill the insight and inspiration to help the students. Let the sets and costumes that the school creates be things of beauty that would attract you and attract others to you. We commit the dramas of the school to you. In Jesus' name. Amen.

November 17: Art. Loving Father, caring Father, we thank you for blessing creation with beauty and proportion, that we may reflect in art devoted to you. Thank you for blessing the school with art teachers, creative volunteers, and students who have a heart, mind, and skill for creating things of beauty. Accept the offerings

of the students in art as devoted to you, with whatever skill they have. Increase their skill, discipline, and devotion to the arts, so that they may create things of beauty calling attention to you. Let their art be devoted not to themselves or to idols but to you, as seen in the subjects and in the execution. Encourage the art teachers that they have a valued ministry within the school. Let your praise reach the students who make art for you. In Jesus' name. Amen.

November 18: Music. God of Israel, God of All, we celebrate your glory, your eminence, your beauty, your righteousness, your love, and your salvation in song. Help the school choir and band learn the skill of singing and playing instruments to your glory and for your worship. Give each singer and musician the discipline, sensitivity, understanding, ear, and devotion to make music that honors you and calls others to join in your worship. Hear the song of the children of the school lifted up in your praise and accept their offering with a glad heart. Encourage the choir and band leaders, the parents, and the students themselves that you love the music of the students of the school. We thank you for bringing gifted instructors and blessing the students with their own gifts of song. In Jesus' name. Amen.

November 19: Reverence. Father of Heavenly Lights, of light rather than darkness, of victory rather than defeat, of liberty rather than slavery, and of love rather than hate, we give you glory and honor and praise for all good within the community of the school. That is our prayer today, simply to honor you, revere you, credit you with everything good that occurs for every student within the school and, as an extension, for every family of every student of the school. Your Spirit carries the word, the instruction, the faith, the desire for every student to learn and obey. You are the one who makes the school work, who carries its mission forward, who provides for its operational needs, and who leads the board in governing the school. You are the reason the school exists and the one to whom the school dedicates its mission. And you are fully capable of doing all the school needs to carry out that mission in pursuit of you. We thank you for all who you are and all that you do. In Jesus' name we pray. Amen.

November 20: Technology. God of Glory, all sufficient, all knowing, all seeing, we love you and embrace you and follow you. Help us to see the evil that can come through smartphones, the internet, tablets, and other technologies, and help us to teach the students and families of the school to guard against those evils. The opposer will use any tool, and a tool that can bring temptations and distractions to the very hand of any student of the school is a potential tool of destruction. Lift the students' eyes from distracting and tempting devices into relationships with you and with others. Teach the staff and parents of the school to regulate the use of these devices, and help the staff and parents of the school teach the students to ward off the temptations and distractions of the devices. Place the devices only in the hands of those students who are prepared to guard against their evils. In Jesus' name. Amen.

November 21: Christian Education. Father of Lights, Son of Glory, we trust you so completely that we have given our children to you, knowing that only under you and in you and protected by you will our children live as you would have them do, eternally in paradise with you. Thank you for Christian education, where parents can entrust their children to schools that turn the students not to secular and godless ways that will lead to their enslavement and destruction but to you, to your comfort, to your healing, to your command, and to your flourishing. Thank you for the school and for the families who include alumni of the school. Thank you for blessing the lives of the parents and grandparents who graduated from the school and sent their children to the school in the hopes that those children would also know and love you. Strengthen and protect the school, so that it may continue to welcome the children of alumni and may continue to give children back to you rather than to a world that does not love them. In Jesus' name. Amen.

> **Relevance.** Prayer has powerful positive effects on the one who engages in it. One of those effects is to heighten the awareness of the one who prays as to the relevance of things in that person's life. When one addresses God, one ought not bring trivialities to the address. Speaking to God helps one choose subjects carefully, for their significance.

November 22: Next Generation. Dear Holy One, you have drawn us out of our own slavery and the slavery of those who would use and abuse us. You have brought us out of Egypt once again, another generation raised up to love you and to live in your liberty. We ask that you raise up out of the school the next generation to love you, to love your liberty, and to live in communion with you, free of Egypt's enslavement, free of tyranny. Don't let the world take the school's children, turning them away from you. Instead, let the students of the school benefit from its instruction and the protection and instruction of their parents, so that they are the next generation to walk out of Egypt with you. In Jesus' name. Amen.

November 23: Adversary. Father God, you who slay the giants, who topple the adversary, who remove the oppressor, and who free the enslaved. We are in awe of your strength in battle and your victories over the strong who oppose you. Topple the giants who stand in opposition to the school and the instruction of its students in your way and word. Destroy the oppressor who enslaves the heart of

the students and makes them unable to hear and embrace your word. Slay the dragons who stand between the students and you, between the students and learning more of your word. Enlist the staff and students of the school in your righteous army, so that when you go out to battle, the staff and students fight with you and not against you. Let us see those giants fall, whether they are inside us or outside of us. In Jesus' name. Amen.

November 24: Worship. Lord and Savior, Almighty God, we worship you, we revere you, we celebrate you whenever two or more of us gather. You give us the joy, hope, and promise we need to persevere in your creation, broken by our sin, corrupted in its holy character. Help the staff members of the school to cultivate a culture of worship in all that the school does, to foster in the spirit of the school's students a sense of worship. Make the worship gatherings at the school rich in love and inspiration, but above all, satisfying to you. Let the praises of the students of the school go up to you, out of hearts in earnest. For we know that worship is our first place, our first resort, for all that we hope and do. You are worthy of our worship. Give us hearts to worship you. In Jesus' name. Amen.

November 25, 2023: Culture. Holy Father, blessed Son, you reign supreme over all creation. You are the creator of all that is good. And your holiness stands powerfully apart. Do not let the culture of the world inhabit and transform the school, but let your Spirit instead inhabit and transform the school's culture. Let the school be so different in its righteousness and holiness, its humility and gentleness, its order and respect, that anyone who enters instantly knows it. Then help the teachers show the students how to take your Spirit to the dinner table, the playground, and eventually to the workplace and business place and government, to transform the culture there in the image of Christ. Make the graduates of the school into culture transformers rather than those who adopt the broken culture of the world without you. In Jesus' name. Amen.

November 26: Build and Struggle. Father God, you who are both a builder and a fighter, using the tools of service and the sword of truth, to build up the social structures and institutions that serve you and benefit your people, while using the sword of truth to bring down things that oppose you and oppress your people. We need your strength and your courage. We need your shovel and your sword. Help the school to teach its students, your children sent by families devoted to you, both to build and to fight, to use both the shovel and the sword. Equip them for service in your world, with the tools and weapons that you require them to wield. Put the sword of truth in their mouths and the helmet of salvation over their heads, together with the breastplate of righteousness against all attacks. In Jesus' name. Amen.

> **Simplicity.** Your daily school prayer need not convince God with the prayer's sophistication. When you pray, you are not reasoning, arguing, or justifying. You are certainly not impressing God with how articulate or fancy your prayers sound. Keep your words simple. It is enough when his heart and your heart align.

November 27: Victory. Holy Father, we stand in awe and respect for your victory over the opposer and all that is evil in the world. You are the judge of all and the victor over all and will stand in the end against all that opposes your way and your word and your people. Help the school to stand with you and to stand against those who oppose you.

Help the staff members of the school to teach the students to struggle not just against the flesh but against the powers and principalities that oppose you and oppress your people. Help the students become graduates of the school who take your struggle into the institutions in which they live, work, and serve, to uplift your way and life as a model for righteousness. Help them become victors, too, humble enough to stand for you and your word when others oppose it. In Jesus' name. Amen.

November 28: Cultivation. Father of Lights, Father of Glory, we turn to you as our only hope, as our only refuge, as our only source of all that is good. We thank you for sharing your word and way and truth and life so completely, utterly, richly, and constantly. Help the students and staff and community of the school to cultivate your fields, to sow often and widely and deeply the seeds of your holy word, in soil that is rich and broken up and ready for growth, and then to tend the fields consistently and with discipline and devotion so that you bring forth a harvest of righteousness in individual lives, in friendships, in marriages, in homes, and in communities. Show the students of the school what a life cultivated with devotion to your word and way looks like. Bring models of Christian living before the students so that they may emulate those models while discovering their own identity and their own field in which to work for you. In Jesus' name. Amen.

November 29: Application. Father God, our creator, inspiration, counselor, hope, and guide, help the teachers of the school teach the students to apply your good news to their life, to see how your word moves and lives among them, to take what they learn from you and of you and give it form in the way they move through the world. Let the application of your word be to every circumstance. Let the students of the school see how practical your word is, how it makes constant differences in their lives. And then help them to turn away from their many pursuits that are not according to your principles and patterns so that they may turn toward your good news, to shape good and purposeful and meaningful lives. In Jesus' name. Amen.

November 30: Institutions. Dear God, the architect of all that is orderly and good, the one who sanctions our social and spiritual structures like marriage, church, and the school, guides our government and military, informs our businesses and ministries, and builds fair and just and necessary institutions, we give you the credit for all that brings benefit and flourishing. You are our rock and foundation. We have no other. When we ignore your word and command, these institutions fail. We thank you for giving us institutions that are imbued with your principles and patterns, for they are the only institutions that would serve us and serve you well. Raise up the students of the school to lead those institutions, social, governmental, charitable, and religious. Make these students grounded so deeply in you that their faith informs and shapes the institutions within which they live, learn, work, and serve. Help our staff to see and teach the role of your word in giving ground to these institutions, for our only hope and future is in you. In Jesus' name. Amen.

December 1: Eighth Graders. Dear Heavenly Father, we pray today for the eighth graders of the school, for their coming graduation, that they will prepare statements of their belief in thanks and in truth about your goodness and care and compassion. Keep them secure in your love and secure in the faith, with your word as their lamp and your commands as their honor. Protect them, and help them to reach adulthood with the purity and righteousness you desire for our youth. Prepare them to form and lead and serve their own families in the coming years. But above all hold them close to you. Let their class be a credit to you and to the school and its staff. Thank you for every one of them. In the name of Jesus. Amen.

December 2: Seventh Graders. Father God, we pray for the seventh graders of the school, that they enter this next stage in their development toward adulthood prepared to carry your word in their heart, to continue to embrace and trust and rely on you. The world may open to them in a way that tempts them to ignore you. Let that not be so. Confirm them in the faith that they may continue to adore and serve and obey you. Help the staff members shepherd these seventh graders through the curriculum and toward high school, carrying your word like a flame in their hearts, guiding and counseling and protecting them, even nourishing them in their development, relationships, and witness to your glory. In Jesus' name we ask. Amen.

December 3: Legacy. Oh dear God, we thank you for the legacy of the school, living on its graduates, now three, four, or more generations from the current students you have entrusted to the school. We thank you for their witness to your goodness and to the goodness of instruction in your word. We treasure this legacy, holding it up as our model, and asking that you help us preserve it and amplify it and pass it on to the next generation of students, staff members, and volunteers of the school. This legacy of the school is yours, to your credit and honor and for your glory, seen in the lives and righteousness of its graduates. Let this legacy live on in testimony to your care and goodness. In Jesus' name we pray. Amen.

> **Attention.** We pursue and become that about which we think. One of the more powerful effects of prayer is to concentrate the mind on important subjects. The adversary makes every effort to distract us, efforts with which our flesh is quite willing to comply. Prayer counteracts that deadly effect. See your time of prayer as inoculation against the adversary's deadly efforts.

December 4: Advent. Our Heavenly Father, you who care so deeply for your children, for the students of the school and for their families, as well as for the staff, we ask in this Advent season your peace on every child, family, staff member, and volunteer in the school community. Let this season be one of quiet assurance, of simple hope, of plain humility before you, the great God and provider, in whose hands all things good are available for us, if we would only ask and wait. We implore you to give us your peace and rest in this special season remembering your coming so long ago but yet so recently, for your Spirit reminds us of that special day and hour when you entered the world to redeem us with your life given on the cross. We accept, embrace, and honor your gift of life, of restoration, even of resurrection from the dead to eternal life in your paradise kingdom. In Jesus' name we pray. Amen.

December 5: Rest. Heavenly Father, Righteous Son, and Holy Spirit, we pray today that you would give rest and restoration to the students, staff, and volunteers of the school over the coming Christmas break. Give the students,

staff, and their families peace, time together, time apart, enjoyment, and new energy with which to start the new year. Let minds be cleared of old issues and old offenses, so that returning to school feels fresh, like a new beginning. And let staff members and students return with new commitment, new ideas, and the perseverance that teaching and learning takes. In Jesus' name. Amen.

December 6: Reorganization. Father God, we commit to you the organization and reorganization of the staff and administration of the school. We acknowledge that the blessing of growth of the school has brought challenges with the staff and administration keeping up. We discern the need for additional staff and for reorganizing the staff to the greatest effect. Help us to discern your way of doing so, valuing every staff member, placing them in the best position to use their gifts, and serving all students of the school. Give the school leader your insight, and let the board and its committees help the leader see your will. Give the school the financial means to increase staffing to accomplish the school's mission to instruct in your word to raise up graduates committed to serving you. In Jesus' name. Amen.

December 7: Student Services Staff. Holy Father, we pray today for the student services staff of the school, for those brave souls who manage the problems the school faces in keeping students healthy enough to learn as they need to do. We admit the brokenness of families and students, their limitations and challenges, and how those conditions affect their ability to learn in the way you would have them do. We acknowledge the special dedication special needs require from the student services staff. Give those staff members those skills, equipping them to serve and support students with special needs. Give those staff members the strength, insight, and dedication, as well as the respect of the teachers and leaders of the school. And then heal the disabilities and correct the conditions affecting learning in the school. We ask in Jesus' name. Amen.

December 8: Finances. Lord Jesus Christ and Holy Father, we pray today for the school's finances, its budget, its endowment, and its ability to sustain its operations including adequately compensating its staff. We also pray for the financial welfare of the school's families. We know how hard it is for families to pay to send students to the school. Thank you for giving those families the means and the hearts, indeed the trust and confidence, to send students to the school. Give the families the jobs and income they need to continue to do so. Help the school manage its finances to ensure their stability without loss and with full confidence of the families of the school. Grow the endowment. Attract further donors to it. And thank you for moving the hearts and providing the means for donors to contribute. Relieve the burden of tuition on the families, but also show them the rewards of their commitment to the instruction of their children at the school. Help the school to provide them with the value they need to see in the faith, growth, and learning of their students. In Jesus' name. Amen.

> **Interest.** Your daily school prayers need not attempt to capture God's interest. He already cares for you far more than you can imagine anyone caring. Pray with confidence that he was already waiting for you to speak to him, with great interest and attention. Remember how he gave his Son for you, proving the extreme level of his interest.

December 9: Sixth Graders. Father God, we pray for the sixth graders of the school, for their continued growth, learning, and commitment to you. You have raised them up to an age when they can know you as their own, not as their parents would, but through their own exploration of your word and receipt of your Spirit. Help the staff members and volunteers of the school lead the sixth graders to a relationship with you, through your Son Jesus Christ. Give the sixth graders the peace they need, as their minds and bodies develop. Give them the patience they need with themselves and one another. And give them a heart for righteousness in their transition through childhood toward life as a youth and before long as an adult. Let the parents trust the staff to instruct and discipline them in your way. And give them a heart for you. In Jesus' name. Amen.

December 10: Life. Oh, Holy One, you hold the keys to life. Your word is our only reason, our only hope, our only way of living with purpose and efficacy. Your word tells us to live without you is to live in futility, ignorance, and darkness. We don't want darkness for the students of the school. We don't want them to grow up believing that they can make no difference in their world. And so open their hearts and minds to your word so that they can lead flourishing lives of meaning, purpose, and effect. We ask in Jesus' name. Amen.

December 11: God's Will. Father God, we have one prayer today, which is to reveal to us your will for the school. Show each of us, the students, staff members, volunteers, families, donors, and partners of the school what you have for us, large and small, to do. Open the door and provide the means for us to fulfill your every desire for the school. Let every word of instruction be the right word to open the students' minds and hearts to you. Let every act of administration be the right act to organize, guide, and support the school. Let every act of service promote your will. Teach us to do right for the school in all we do. And then take your due honor and credit for every success of the school, for every student's graduation from the school, for every student moving up each grade in the school, for each step forward in the school's mission in service of you. In Jesus' name. Amen.

December 12: Board Wisdom. Jesus Christ our Lord, and Holy Father, we pray together for the wisdom of the board of the school. Unite us in vision, in fellowship, in love for you our Almighty God and source of all knowledge and understanding. Unite us in love for the students of the school. Unite us in support of the school's leader and staff. Unite us in commitment to the growth of the school. Unite us in faith in your way and your word, in our trust in the proximity of your kingdom. For indeed, you are very near. You are in our own hearts, guiding us and constituting us as a governing board. Help us not to interfere but to support and serve, and to govern and guide and hold accountable when necessary, but always in gentleness and kindness and respect. Bring to the board the voice and insight and experience and gifts of every member, expressed for the good of the school and the wisdom of the board's actions, always in line as you, oh Lord, desire and will. Forgive the board of its every offense, for we have need of your mercy in all we are and all we do. And shower your blessing on each board member and the family of each board member for the good service they do, all in your will. In Jesus' name we pray. Amen.

December 13: School Leader. Lord and Savior, Author of life and all that is good, we pray today for our school leader, that he would know that you carry his mantle, lift his burdens, care for his health, love his children, support his marriage, and call him forward in pursuit of you in the ministry he serves within the school. Strengthen our school leader. Give him your vision. Bless him with your

wisdom. Give him your own faith. And give him the voice of reason and blessing and comfort and instruction. Help him to equip the staff for its precious work among the students of the school, shaping hearts and educating minds for you. Show our school leader your mercy and grace in his failings, and show him your favor in his service as his reward. Help the board to treat him with the value and respect he deserves as your servant in this special ministry of instructing the young. Strengthen his relationships with the school's families and the school's community partners. And let your light shine through him, into the students, staff, families, volunteers, and partners of the school. In Jesus' name we pray. Amen.

December 14, 2023: Church Neighbor. Father God, we pray for the school's neighbor church, for its ministry among God's people, for its pastor, for its congregation, and for its witness to your incomparable word and work in saving us as your people. Bring new families to its membership, new finances to its accounts, and new energies to its ministries of service and care. Raise up its people in your own righteousness, that they may flourish while shining your light among those who don't know you and need to learn of your love and glory. Strengthen the partnership between the school and its neighbor church, over the grounds and facilities it so generously lends the school, the chapel services its pastor provides, the use of its sanctuary for students to worship, and in every other opportunity that the school and church may work together in your kingdom. In Jesus' name. Amen.

> **Concentration.** Concentration is spectacularly hard in today's screen-driven world. Treasure your time in daily school prayer, as training in concentration. Concentrated thought helps us see what God has for us and desires from us.

December 15: Order. Heavenly Father, you who are the architect and determiner of beauty, in your perfect proportion and breathtaking design. We glory in the beauty of your creation and the way in which you have made the school a reflection of that glory. We see in the plumb walls and attractive roof lines, the green grass and trimmed shrubbery, the new and old plantings, and the stained-glass windows of the library, a reflection of your goodness, how you balance and proportion all things, how you are the God of order and design. But we also don't trim the shrubs too tightly or demand other perfections in the order of your gifts because we know that you have mercy for the boundaries, for the people and things that dwell just beyond the bounds of your kingdom, that you would wish to make them yours as well. And so, help us to appreciate your design and beauty in the voices of the singing students, their dramatic representation of your story, and all that you have given the school. In Jesus' name we pray. Amen.

December 16: Building. Oh, Holy One, of the heavenly lights and all glory and righteousness, we thank you for blessing the school with the property and buildings necessary to carry out the school's mission in pursuit of you. Thank you for every acre, every wall, every furnishing, and all the physical plant that makes the school possible. We appreciate the security from harm the door locks provide the students, the shelter of the roof and walls, the

heat of the boiler, and the light of the windows and utilities. We thank you for water and power, for bright paint and colorful carpet, and for lockers and chairs and whiteboards and desks. We thank you also for the generosity of the families who have sacrificed so that the school would enjoy these buildings and grounds and furnishings and utilities. We thank you also for the devotion of the volunteers

and staff and vendors who care for the facility, cleaning, repairing, and maintaining it. Now continue to provide for it and keep it in good shape, as we accept the responsibility to steward this gift from you. In Jesus' name we pray. Amen.

December 17: Forgiveness. Father God, forgive every leader, staff member, volunteer, student, and family of the school for every offense against you. Show your mercy to every member of the school community. We are all under the blood of your Son Jesus Christ. Keep us secure in our salvation so that we may live eternally with you. Show us where we need to repent, and then give us the strength and discipline to do so. Do not let us go on sinning against you. But do not punish us as we deserve lest we have nothing left for you. Your Son took our punishment, due only to us, and we acknowledge his payment in full gratitude. Help us also to forgive others because we know that you only forgive us as we forgive others. Give us the soft heart and humility necessary to know that we do not judge others in the way that you do. In Jesus' name. Amen.

December 18: Wonders. Dear God, dear Father, oh Holy One, so high above us, so deep, so profound, so awe-inspiring, possessed of so many wonders, show the school those wonders, opening the hearts and minds of its students to explore and investigate and welcome and embrace you. Give every student of the school a hunger to know your every word, to see your every movement, and to pursue you with the desire you have for us. Give the students of the school your faith, your perseverance, and your discipline, so that they may see and draw from your beauty, your grace, and your strength. In Jesus' name. Amen.

December 19: Glory. Heavenly Father, we are once again before your throne, at the foot of the cross, in need of you and your glory. The school would be nowhere and nothing without your continual presence, without your constant provision, without your Spirit walking its halls. We want to see your glory shine over the school so that its students may shine your light into their own hearts and souls, in their families, and in their communities. Bless the staff with the inspiration of your word and Spirit so that they may instruct the students in your way. Help the staff know the words and actions to take to show your love and teach your principles and patterns, so that these students may recognize you and see all that you desire for them. You are so constant with us, so persevering, and for that, we love and honor you. In Jesus' name. Amen.

December 20: Blessing. Father, Son, and Holy Spirit, our triune God, as a board we ask that you continue to bless the school students, families, staff, leader, and volunteers. Shower them with your mercy, grace, and love. Guide them with your word and Spirit. Comfort them with your presence. Forgive them for their wrongs. You are not only able but also desire to do good for the school community. And you have done good, bringing the school to a point of flourishing. We thank you for every grace. Continue to provide so that the school may do as you will. In Jesus' name. Amen.

December 21: Mercy. God our Father, you are the author of light, we know on this darkest of days, the winter solstice. You are the one who opens our eyes, warms our heart, brings forth the plants and flowers, feeds the animals, nourishes the earth with your rains, brings forth the harvest. We do not deserve any of this provision, for we stumble in the darkness of our broken hearts. Forgive us for hardening our hearts and turning our face away from you, when you invite us into your own heart and turn your own face toward us. We thank you for every mercy and each small and large grace. You have blessed the school so richly, so many times pulling it out of the mire and into the light of your blessing. Do so again, for we have every need for you. Move heaven and earth to give the school's staff your words, your heart for every student of the school. Break the hard hearts and rebellious spirits of students who do not know their own sin. Show every student their need for repentance and to turn to you, obeying your word. Give the staff the courage and sensitivity and skill to discipline the students in exactly the way that will benefit them most. We ask these things in Jesus' name.

December 22: Sustaining Grace. Father God, thank you for walking with every staff member this Fall, for supporting every family, for embracing every student, for opening every door, for securing every hour, for safety, warmth, food, supplies, shelter, play, learning, and every other service you have provided this Fall to keep the school community serving its mission in pursuit of you. We give

you all the credit, knowing that without your nourishment, mercy, love, and care, the school would be nothing. You have sustained the school through more than a century of ministry in the instruction of the city's young in your way and your word, and for that consistency and care, we give you honor, glory, and credit. We owe it all to you, credit it to your grace, and give you the praise you so richly and utterly deserve. Thank you, Lord, for the ministry of the school. May you continue to bless the school in the coming calendar year. In Jesus' name. Amen.

December 23: Hearts. Father, we know your heart for us, your own image, and for the rest of your good creation, a heart so gentle and humble that you gave your Son's life, pouring out his heart to redeem us and the world, to restore us to your heart where our eternal residence is. We confess the hardness of our own hearts resisting your word to follow our own desires, while admitting also that the students in our care have similar hearts. We thank you that you are willing to give us and the school's students new hearts, and we ask that you do so not against our will but because we desire it as the only hope we and the school's students have to know you and to flourish here and in your coming kingdom. In Jesus' name we ask. Amen.

December 24: Advent. As the eve of the celebration of your Son Jesus Christ's birth, his advent, is here upon us, we wonder at the glory of this history you have given us, that you would enter the world not to rule it but to redeem it, for you have ruled it from the beginning, and you will rule it in the end, but we have broken it so that it needed your redemption. We marvel at your advent through the humble mother of God, in the lowest place, with the lowest station, though you are our King of kings, exalted higher than any authority, indeed the creator and delegator of all authority. Forgive us for forgetting our heritage in you, that you were our Father from the beginning, that you stand prepared to adopt us again as your sons and daughters as we embrace your own Son Jesus Christ. Forgive when we have failed to instruct your children as you would have us do so, and show us mercy as you show the students of the school mercy for their own brokenness and wrongs. Bless the students of the school and their families this advent eve and through these holidays into the new year and beyond into eternity. Give us your peace and rest. We give you the glory that was yours from the beginning of the world. In Jesus' name. Amen.

December 25: Redemption. O Holy One, Father of Glory, Son of Righteousness, Beacon of Light, we know no other good than you and what you have brought forth from your own creation. We know no other Savior than your own Son Jesus Christ, who is our only way, hope, truth, and life. We have no hope other than in you. Forgive us for placing our trust in other things, other ways, for we have only one Savior in you. Forgive us for our self-reliance, our pride, and our running after other things than those things you would have us enjoy in you. We thank you for offering your very Son and, in your Son, everything you have in you. We thank you for offering us redemption and restoration, which we accept through confession of our sin and embrace of your Son's sacrifice and his blood in payment for our own wrongs. We thank you for blessing the school. We thank you for lights and heating and furniture and texts and all the things you have provided so that the students of the school may learn more about you. Our prayer is that you continue to bless the school, its staff, its leader, its volunteers, and all those who contribute to its mission in pursuit of you. Keep the lights on, the staff paid and healthy, the roof secure, the physical plant functioning, and above all your Spirit richly involved in everything the school does. In Jesus' name. Amen.

> **Relationships.** Another of prayer's powerful salutary effects is to improve your relationships, not just with God, which of course is your most important relationship, but with family members, friends, and others. Guard your time of daily school prayer as feeding and improving your relationships. Prayer is setting your spirit right, from which those around you benefit.

December 26: Desire. Father God, creator of all, and whose all creation is good, we revere you, knowing you not only as our maker but also as our provider, as our comfort, as our Savior, and even as our companion and friend. We see in your work in the school the blessing of your desire, the beauty of your order, the devotion of your heart, and the service of your hands. We admit our forgetfulness, our waywardness, and our distraction, when we do not think of you, rely on you, beseech you, and honor you as we should. Forgive us, Father, for we are sinners and we sin. But we thank you for your mercy in not treating us as we deserve but instead as you desire. We thank you for providing and guiding the board, the leadership, and the staff of your school. We thank you for bringing families here who trust our care for and teaching of their children. And we ask that you give us not only the skills and strength but also the heart to fulfill that trust and to enrich the lives and spirits of these children with your love, your holy word, and your Holy Spirit. In Jesus' name. Amen.

December 27: Coming Year. Holy Father, you who bring light, truth, hope, and love, shining in our darkness, showing us your way, we stand in awe of your goodness, your consistency, your devotion to our salvation, and your desire that we know you. We confess the hardness of our hearts, the depths of our ignorance of your ways, and how we have failed to hear all that you would share with us if we would only listen. We thank you for what you have said and what we have received from you out of your love and sacrifice. We thank you for sending your Son as your way to rejoin you in paradise, the security and glory of your kingdom. And we ask that you bless the school again this coming calendar year as you have blessed it every year since you established it in the heart of this city so long ago. We ask that you help the board to be the stewards you would have us be of the school's precious mission and that through our humility and devotion to you the school would flourish under your rule in this next calendar year. In Jesus' name. Amen.

December 28: Perseverance. Oh, Lord and Savior, you who brought us out of the darkness through the loving example, service, teaching, and sacrifice of your only Son Jesus Christ, our Messiah, we humble ourselves before you, bowing in honor of your truth and love, as our very creator and sustainer, the author of our own life and provider of everything on which we depend. Forgive us, Father, for the many sins we have committed against one another, our very brothers and sisters, in the hardness of our hearts, under the deceptions of our adversary. Forgive us for not leading and serving as you would have us do, so that your school may be the beacon of your light for which you established it so long ago. We thank you for persisting with us and with the school so faithfully and richly, despite our

obvious failings. We thank you for your word and how you have permitted the school's leader and staff to share your word with so many students and their families, with such inspiration and to such good effect as your Spirit moves with delight through those families and into the community. We only ask that you double the portion of your Spirit you pour out on the school so that your Spirit would overflow to the point of raising the school again as a light to the community and world. Send the school's students into the world carrying your word and light, attracting the interest and devotion of others. In Jesus' name. Amen.

December 29: Healing. Almighty God, you who divided the heavens from the earth, separated land from the waters, and made the flora and fauna for us to steward and enjoy, even before giving us the breath of life. We have forgotten all that you do for us, needing your constant reminder. We have filled our days with activities, without remembering your breath of life. Show us your mercy again, as you do every day, every hour, so that we have the heart to turn again to you to give you the honor you are due. We thank you for that mercy, shown so utterly in your willing sacrifice of your own Son, to restore us to our heritage with you and to redeem the broken world. Restore all things, resurrect the dead, bring life and renewal across the land and within the school. Especially this day, give rest, relief, and restoration for the school's staff, burdened with so many responsibilities, challenged by some many duties, and all while facing the sicknesses, anxieties, and depressions so common in the world today. Bring the staff back to the school after this break with new energy and restored commitment, with new love for the students and inspiration of the Spirit, so that the school may do the good work you have for it to do in educating minds and shaping hearts for service to you. In Jesus' name. Amen.

December 30: Word. Fearsome God, loving Provider, and gracious Savior, we see how beneficently you rule, how gently you draw us out of our captivity, how surely you restore our spirits and renew our souls. You strike awe in our spirit, and we humble ourselves before you accordingly. Forgive us every arrogance of our own, every sleight when we claim credit due you or due others, and

every insult and offense we give to our brothers and sisters in Christ. Thank you for not holding us accountable for all our many wrongs but instead forgiving our sins through the blood of your Son Jesus Christ. Thank you for ordering the school according to your will and righteousness, and for raising up this next generation of spiritual leaders to go forward in testimony to you. Give the school's staff the insight and inspiration of your Spirit into the meaning and significance of your word, to share those lessons richly with the school's students, that they may carry those lessons home where they would both receive and spread your Spirit. Bless the day, the school, its students, and today especially the school's staff to do as you will and desire, for your glory and credit. In Jesus' name. Amen.

December 31: New Year. Gentle Father, you who draw us so surely and so lovingly, while sparing the punishment we are so deservedly due, you have carried out that punishment on your own Son for our redemption and the redemption of the world. We give you every glory, every credit for all good in this world, especially the good service that our own hands find to do for you and with you and in your strength and Spirit. Confessing our need for you, we ask again that you would show us your mercy by overlooking our wrongs and seeing instead in us the image and work of your own Son Jesus Christ who is our Lord and who we know you raised to life again to restore him to your own throne, as the Lamb slain before the world began, in whom we find all reason. Our request on this day is that you open your new year shining your glory over the school, that every student, parent, guardian, staff member, leader, volunteer, and guest would know your eminence, the very goodness of your holy rule. Father, make this new calendar year a new day, a new spirit in your own Holy Spirit, a time of renewal and growth and recommitment to all that is good and holy and pure in you. In this new year, shower your abundance on the school's finances that the school may grow as you would have it grow. Open the hearts of the benefactors of this school who see in its work the desire you have for the school, to spread your light into the hearts of all those who don't yet know you. Expand the school's influence and enrollment and service in witness of the power and love you hold. In Jesus' name. Amen.

January 1: New Blessings. Holy Father, our hearts join with you, to listen, speak, and share your love with you. We have only you and value nothing but what you provide. You are our hope and future, and our comfort and provision, too. Forgive us when we pursue anyone or anything other than you. Forgive us for making idols of even those gifts you give us to enjoy and use. Extend your mercy again, Lord, for our only salvation is in you. Let this new year show your mercy and grace in the darkest places, where all seems lost without your rescue. In this new year, bring to the school the funds, plans, and other resources necessary to pursue the mission of the school in the way you would have us do. Let the ground break for new classrooms, let the plans be exciting, stimulating new hope and confidence in the school. Let the workers be skilled. Then bring new families to the school to commit their children to instruction in your way, filling new classrooms, and learning with excitement about you. Nourish the spirits and energies of the staff, protect the school's leader, and give your vision to the school's board and donors. Move the school forward according to your will, for your glory. In the name of your glorious Son Jesus. Amen.

January 2: Protection. Heavenly Father, you whom we revere, we desire, we praise, your love astounds us. Your generosity toward us overflows. We know that you have rewards for us in heaven so far greater than the rewards we seek on earth that earthly rewards are rusted, corroded, worthless in comparison. How much higher you are, how much better your kingdom is, and how much we desire you. But we confess that we haven't acted as we know we should. We have pursued things here, stolen your honor, and refused your better gifts. Forgive us for our shortsightedness, for our dishonesty, for our offenses against you and others. Our salvation is solely in you, as we stand at the foot of the cross, receiving the sacrificed blood of your own Son as our redemption, his payment for our own wrongs. We only ask that you protect the school from the wiles and deceptions of our awful adversary, from the deception, too, of our own hearts. Help us this year to hear and honor and obey your word. Help us to educate the students entrusted to the school by faithful parents and by parents seeking faith. Help the students grow, not just by the necessary year but by leaps and bounds in their capacity to know and embrace you, while serving others in the name of your Son Jesus Christ. We ask these things in that very name Jesus. Amen.

> **Proximity.** When you pray your daily school prayer, know how near God is to you. You need not shout or announce your prayers, as if calling to God in another room. He is not just right beside you. He is in you, in your heart, in the deepest reaches of your mind. You are speaking to him from the depths of your soul. He hears you before you even form the words in your mind or express them from your lips.

January 3: Confession. Father of Lights, Father of Glory, Father of Peace, we adore you and only you, not the gifts you give us, which we appreciate, but the giver of those gifts, you. We move our hearts toward you, joining you where you would have us be, under your wing, in your shelter, in your house, in your kingdom, under your rule, at your foot, listening, hearing, accepting your desires as our own, your will as our own, your heart as our own. We confess that these are our commitments but that they go unfilled. We do not listen and hear, we hear but do not accept, we know what you will but follow our own. Correct us, Father, but do so gently, mercifully, as you would sons and daughters, for that is who we are, your adopted, your chosen, your redeemed under the blood of your glorious Son Jesus Christ. These are our wishes for every student of the school, that they would be yours in heart, desire, will, and obedience. We ask in Jesus' name. Amen.

January 4: Faith. Father God, you of gentle and humble heart, while also of supreme power and our judge, your glory reigns, your honor shines like the sun, your credit is on our lips and in our hearts, for we have no other Savior, no other guide, no other father, no other hope than you. Our minds are so limited, our hearts so deceptive, our hands so distracted, and our feet so weak, that we do not

know what to think, what to desire, what to grasp, or how to stumble forward in pursuit of you. Give us strength, renew our devotion, fill our minds, and change our hearts so that we follow you. Bless every student, staff member, family, and volunteer of this school with the same strength, devotion, understanding, and desire that you have for your chosen, for those whom you redeemed with the sacrifice and confession of your Son who is our Lord Jesus Christ. Strengthen especially on this day the staff of the school to do your will instructing these children in your way. We ask in Jesus' name. Amen.

January 5: Confession. God in heaven, God of earth, God of all things, supreme, sovereign, eternal, uncreated, holy, both beyond and here, we adore and revere you above all things. We have no one other than you. Forgive us for every oversight and omission as a board of the school, when we have failed to discern your will and failed to pursue the righteousness you set before us. Forgive us for every distraction we have entertained when you were calling and guiding. Forgive us for hard hearts and closed ears and absent spirits. We kneel at the foot of the cross, receiving your Son's payment for our every wrong, knowing that we have no other grounds on which to receive your mercy. Thank you for giving us this ministry of yours to tend, to shepherd, and for which to pray and humble ourselves before you to receive your blessing and provision. Thank you for moving the hearts of the donors, the leader, the staff, and the volunteers. Thank you for every family and for each student. We ask that you shape the hearts and instruct the minds of every student, through every teacher and staff member and volunteer, through the pastors who support the school, through your own Spirit. Strengthen the staff and leader, guide the board, move the hearts of the donors and volunteers, and provide, provide, provide for your children, these students of the school. In Jesus' name. Amen.

January 6: Daycare. Father God, we care for the children of this community and their working families. We hear of a local church's need to no longer operate a daycare ministry and the church's desire that the school take it over. We have struggled to discern the role of the school in the matter, seeing that preschool is already a part of the school's ministry in pursuit of its mission, but that infant care is beyond the school's expertise and role. If you desire the school to be involved in some way in the continued provision of daycare services, then open a door, point us in the direction of structure and solution, and give us the location and other means. If you desire the school not to do so, then close the door, and indicate clearly to us our mission and role, while you provide for the families who may lose infant care as a result. These things we ask in Jesus' name. Amen.

January 7: Plans. Heavenly Father, our glorious King, you have placed in our hearts plans to expand the school, not out of pride but out of humility and the desire to serve.

You have increased the school's enrollment to the point that the school is running out of classrooms and cannot gather the whole school for worship in its gym. You have blessed the school with growth. Now provide the financial means for the school to add to its building more classrooms and an auditorium large enough for the whole school community to worship you.

The plans we see must be your plans or they would have no chance of coming to life. Show us your desire for the school, and then give us the means to pursue that desire. We see the opportunity for the school to reach more students and families. We believe doing so is the school's mission after your heart. If that be so, then bring the donors to the school with the heart to bless your plans financially so that construction may begin this year. We ask in Jesus' name. Amen.

January 8: Local Government. Our glorious God and Savior, you have blessed the school with many students, so many that we have special needs to ask of our local government and governing officials. Move the hearts of local government leaders so that your plans for the school, its students, and its safety and security would swiftly go through government approvals and receive government recognition and services where due. Help the school's community to allow local government to equitably and impartially serve the school's needs so that the school may move forward in your will. We ask in Jesus' name. Amen.

January 9: Grace. Heavenly Father, to whom we give all honor, whose glory we regard in the heavens and on earth, whose place above creation has no equal, in whom we trust for all provision, comfort, and salvation, forgive us our wrongs, when we have failed to lead and listen and follow as you desire. Thank you for your abundant, never-ending grace. Thank you for giving us what you desire rather than what we deserve, that you remain steadfast when we abandon you, that your faith continues when we lack faith, and that you forgive under the blood of your Son when we have no merit to claim it. Thank you for blessing the school, for providing for its staff, and for instructing its children. Open student hearts to receive your instruction and words so that they may act as they are, your creations in your image. Give the students minds for instruction in your word. Order the school properly according to your hierarchy and righteousness, and guide the board in governing its mission. Hearten the school's leader. These things we ask in the name of our Lord Jesus Christ. Amen.

> **Gratitude.** Your daily school prayers should improve your stance of gratitude. Asking God for things, even things he desires to give you, makes one appreciate what he has already given you. The more you ask, the more you realize his abundant grace and generosity in having already given without your having asked. As you keep praying daily, see if your gratitude grows.

January 10: Fear. Father God, you who know all things and hold all things, who provide for all needs and protect against all evil, we glorify and praise you with our whole hearts, desiring what you desire and seeking your will in all things. Do not number our errors or count our many wrongs. See us only as covered in the blood of your Son whose payment has redeemed us and draws all things to their order. Protect every student of the school. Let none fear anything other than you, and let that fear of you be of your holiness and righteousness, that all students of the school would know you as you are, so pure and high above as to be without approach, other than in the name and under the covering of our Lord Jesus Christ, who has made us sons and daughters of the Most High. Keep the students of the school in your way. Let them love one another and show the love of Christ in their families and in the community. These things we ask in the name of our Lord Jesus Christ. Amen.

January 11: Compassion. Father God, you who have the gentlest and kindest heart, we want your heart, not our heart. We want our heart to look like your heart, out of which to bring gentleness, kindness, and the Spirit of care, compassion, and love. Give the students of the school your heart so that they may show kindness, gentleness, and joy, first to one another, then to the school's staff and

volunteers, and then to their families and neighbors, and finally to their enemies. Remove our hard hearts, our hearts that seek after our own selves, and replace our hearts with yours. Don't let us be indifferent to others, nor hard and hurtful to others, but kind to others because we have your heart, the heart of Christ. Help our students to care for others, to show the gentleness of Christ and the compassion of one who gave his life for us. And give our teachers and volunteers the heart of Christ as well. These things we ask in Jesus' name. Amen.

January 12: Righteousness. Oh Heavenly Father, if we are honest, we admit that the school community is made of individuals and families with real pain, real suffering, and real problems, not just with life's challenges, but with sin, with unrighteousness, and with brokenness. What the school's students, staff, volunteers, and families need is your healing. We need your relief, your comfort, your compassion, and your strength. We need your renewal, your redemption, your righteousness. We need your mercy, your forgiveness, and your restoration. Every one of us has the same need for you. None are righteous without you. And so, Father God, bring your healing, comfort, and all that we need to carry on toward your kingdom. For we want your kingdom to come on earth, as it is in heaven. We want to live better lives and help others live better lives with us. We have so much need. You know how to meet those needs. In Jesus' name we ask that you do so. Amen.

January 13: Need. Oh, Lord, we know that you are waiting for us to join you. We know that you are not reluctant but eager. We confess that we are the ones who have yet to join you, to turn toward you, and to accompany you. We thank you for your eagerness, your willingness, your patience, and your perseverance with us. If only we would persevere with you. If only we would wait for you. If only we would heed and satisfy your desire for us. Open our ears, our eyes, and our heart to you, Father God. Help us to hear and see you and welcome your desire. The students of the school need you. They have lives to lead that would honor you. They have hopes for a future that is only possible with you. Pour your Spirit out on the staff and volunteers that the students would receive you and walk with you. Bless the school, as you have done. Forgive the school's offenses, as you have also done. Be with us, Lord, for we need you. In Jesus' name we have asked. Amen.

January 14: Healing. Father God, Holy One, the staff of the school suffers illness again. The students are sick with viruses. The volunteers have caught colds. The season is upon us when the darkness and cold weaken us. And as the teachers and volunteers and administrators fight sickness, they lose sight of you. They miss what you have for them to be and to do. Send your healing Spirit, Father. Stop the coughs. Rid the school community of the viruses and disease that burdens it. Shine your healing light in every dark place. Lower the fevers. Strengthen the immune system. Stop the chills. Settle the digestion. Clear the sinuses. Ease the headaches. Restore every student, staff member, and volunteer. For we need you to carry your word into the world. In Jesus' name. Amen.

January 15: Light. Lord Jesus Christ, ruler of heaven and earth, magnificent Savior, Righteous Father and Holy Son, remove from the school every stain and every bit of strife, so that everyone who enters, whether student, parent, staff member, volunteer, vendor, or guest, feels your Spirit comforting, uplifting, sharing your joy, spreading your hope, and removing burdens. Let the school be a beacon of light, drawing everyone into your path, toward your kingdom, toward salvation, and toward living eternally with you. In Jesus' name. Amen.

> **Home.** When you pray your daily school prayers, you are not calling to God in a distant and strange realm. You are speaking with God in your own home, the place for which he made you. Dwell in that place of prayer with as much security, intimacy, comfort, and confidence as you can muster or imagine. When you pray, you are anticipating entering your eternal home.

January 16: Kingdom. Father God, excellent Ruler, Wonderful Counselor, you are a kingdom builder. Your kingdom will come. You have given the school a place in your kingdom, with the role of educating the young in your word, shaping the hearts of its students to love and obey you. Let your kingdom come. Help the school to be the kingdom builder, the kingdom participant, the kingdom witness you desire it to be. Help the board to know how to participate in your work in bringing your heavenly kingdom to earth, even as we prepare to join your kingdom in heaven. In Jesus' name. Amen.

January 17: Preschoolers. Oh Holy and Righteous God, we pray today for the preschoolers, that you would equip and energize the school's wonderful staff members and volunteers to care for the preschoolers, to show them your way, to introduce them to your story, to teach them to love your word, and to obey your commands. Help them to model their young lives on your Son, to be gentle and kind, to care and show compassion for one another and for their family members. Make them gentle to their mother and respectful to their father and kind to their siblings and friends. Strengthen them, develop them, prepare them for first grade and beyond, to fill their greatest capacity for loving you and loving others, even as they love themselves. In Jesus' name. Amen.

January 18: First Graders. Father God, we pray today for the first graders of the school, that they would know you and receive you and love you and learn more of your wondrous love. Help the first-grade teachers and volunteers and parents who care for the school's first graders to show them your love, guide them in your righteousness, show them their need for you in their broken and sinful state, and desire your will. Forgive our first graders every offense, and then raise them up not to continue in their offenses. Show your mercy to our first graders, and help the staff and volunteers teach them their need for your mercy. And protect them this year and in years to come, so that they may grow into the men and women of God you wish them to be. In Jesus' name. Amen.

> **Celebration.** Your daily school prayers should be drawing you into celebrating God more often and deeply. Many of these daily school prayers begin with adoration, as they should. God is worth celebrating. As you pray, celebrate God's love and goodness.

January 19: Volunteers. Heavenly Father, we pray for the volunteers of the school. Make them many. Make them eager to serve. Equip them to serve with the love of your Son. Help them to share your story and know that they are part of your story. Help the volunteers to connect their lives

and their hopes and their prayers with the school and its students and families. Strengthen the volunteers. Then show the volunteers the treasure they have stored up in heaven when serving the school. Welcome the volunteers into your kingdom as your adopted sons and daughters. Embrace the volunteers so that they may know that they have pleased you. Reward them as you would, with the love and comfort and confidence they have in you. And help the school to treat its volunteers with the respect and value the volunteers are due. In Jesus' name. Amen.

January 20: Families. Dear Heavenly Father, we pray for the families of the school. The families of the school face the challenges of every other family, whether in health, employment, housing, food, medical care, and relationships within the home. Ease those challenges. Help each family of the school to overcome those challenges by relying on you and on the gifts you have given them to provide for themselves. Help the school community to share generously the gifts it has, to encourage and support and care for the families of the school. Help the school welcome every family. Help the school show every family it has a place in the school. Let the mothers of the school's students welcome one another and warm one another with their joy for you. Let the fathers of the school's students welcome one another and challenge one another to follow you. Strengthen the marriages of the parents of the students of the school. And forgive those households for every offense against you, that every household may pursue you once again in the confidence that you receive them as your own. In Jesus' name. Amen.

January 21: Story. Father God, oh gentle and humble One, we pray today that you would share your story. Help the staff members and volunteers of the school to teach every student of the school their place in your grand narrative. Show every student that they have a story of their own that reflects and adds to your story. Show them that their story is one of adventure, flourishing, challenge, and success, of warmth, community, and relationship, of hope and a future. Give the school itself a story and remind it of the story with which you have already blessed it so that they can share that story wherever the school's students, parents, staff members, and volunteers go. You are our story. You are our guide. Let us be worthy participants in your account of the heavens and earth. In Jesus' name. Amen.

January 22: Sponsoring Churches. Father God, you of heavenly lights, we pray today for the Spirit of giving, for the sponsoring churches of the school, for their blessing of the school financially and, more so, for their sending of their children to the school to benefit from its instruction.

We pray for the sponsoring churches as partners, thanking you for bringing them to the school and the school to them, to instruct the young in your word and way, while showing your love to all. Strengthen the school's sponsoring churches. Grow their memberships, protect their finances, and vitalize their mission to carry your word to the world. And then bless also the churches of the students of the school, that are not sponsoring churches. Bless those churches, too, with strong leadership, steady finances, and growing memberships. Encourage the churches of the community to entrust the school with their young and to support the school. In Jesus' name. Amen.

> **Rest.** Your daily school prayers can be a time of rest for you. God wants you to rest in him. Your daily school prayers should not be a chore. They should not tire you. They should rejuvenate you for having rested in God. Relax when you pray. Let your mind, body, and breathing slow. You are in God's peace when you pray in his presence.

January 23: Donors. Holy Father, Prince of Peace, King of kings, we pray today for the donors of the school. We thank you for the school's donors, for their trust, their generosity, their confidence in the mission and staff and leadership of the school. Bless the donors. Let them know that their donations are counted not only on earth but also in heaven. Let the donors know that you see their generosity and give them eternal credit, whether others here see it or not. Let them flourish because of their heart for you and for the school. Let their finances grow in recognition of their generosity toward the school. Restore to them double everything that they give to the school. And help the school be good stewards of every dollar each donor gives to the school. Help us to apply those donations for the uses you would have us do. Make us wise and keep us accountable to the donors and to you. In Jesus' name. Amen.

January 24: Rule. Heavenly Father, you who sit so high above us on a throne so glorious in honor of you. You are our authority, you are our sovereign, you are our unquestioned ruler over all we do. The school board, leader, staff, and volunteers give their obedience and commit their citizenship to you. We are first citizens of your kingdom in all we do. Remind us of every responsibility we have as citizens of your kingdom, subject to you. But do not rule us harshly, as an earthly ruler would do. Instead, show us your mercy, even as you share with us your word. But above all let the school be under you, subject to you, guided by you, and ruled by you. Do not let us submit the school to any authority contrary to you. In Jesus' name. Amen.

January 25: Prayer. Dear God of the heavens and the earth, hear our prayer this day and every day. Help us to lift up our requests to you. Let every student of the school ask you for each of their needs. Turn the students to you in prayer. Let their prayers be in honor and adoration of you.

Help the staff members to teach the students to pray in confession to you. Make prayer ring daily throughout the school. And then hear our prayers. Forgive us the sin that would have you turn away from all we ask of you. Help us to confess and repent of our sins, so that you can hear our voice lifted in prayer to you. Make us a praying community at the school. Guide the prayers of every staff member and volunteer, toward your desires, with the motive to please you. We ask these things and every prayer to you in the name of our Lord and Savior Jesus Christ. Amen.

January 26: Second Graders. Father God, we pray today for the second graders of the school. You know how precious these students are to you and to us. You also know how much development they need to do, especially in their hearts for you. Open their hearts to you. Help their teachers and volunteers teach them your way, showing them your way, too. Place your word deep in their hearts so that they may carry your Spirit wherever they go. Protect them. Make them a class of distinction, with joy and warmth and obedience, caring for one another in the way you would have them do. Open their minds to your word and to their lessons, that they would excel academically to carry your gifts into service for you. Make them strong physically and mentally, healing and protecting them as they need from you. Raise them up as your sons and daughters, strong in the faith and secure in you. We ask these things in Jesus' name. Amen.

January 27: Third Graders. Dear Heavenly Father, we pray today for the third graders of the school. Every third grader is precious to you. Make the third-grade class a kind, generous, astute, obedient, and righteous class, with hearts for you. Help their teachers and aides and volunteers and parents to share your word richly with them, so that they may know and embrace and honor you. Give them the nourishment both in your word and in their minds and bodies they need to grow spiritually in you and physically and mentally in service of you. Enlarge their hearts for you, and then fill their hearts with your Spirit so that they may shine with your light in their families and communities and wherever else they go. Make them witnesses to your love. We thank you for them. In Jesus' name. Amen.

> **Secrecy.** God's word encourages secret rather than showy prayer. We know better than to pray in performance. We pray instead in communion with the God who answers our prayers. But the evidence of secret prayer soon becomes apparent. Others see your secret prayer in the calm and joyful spirit your secret prayer fosters within you. Let your daily school prayer in secrecy make your spirit shine in public.

January 28: Fourth Graders. Father God, you who are our only hope and only future, we pray today for the fourth graders of the school, wanting you to know that we have dedicated them to you. Strengthen and guide their teachers, aides, and volunteers to bring your word to them and to show your love to them. As fourth graders, they have so much yet to learn but are also so vital and capable of knowing you. Help them to learn more of you and of the ways of the world, so that they may navigate in the world as you would have them do. Keep them innocent but make them shrewd to avoid the temptations and deceptions of the world. Protect them against the evil one. Send your angels to guard them in all they do. Give them a conscience for you, and then give them the strength and discipline to follow that conscience so that they may please you. In Jesus' name. Amen.

January 29: Fifth Graders. Heavenly Father, on your throne, before your court, in your heavenly paradise, we pray today for the fifth graders of the school. We lift up each fifth grader to you, for only you can protect them and guide them in all they do. Give us the strength and wisdom and insight to teach and serve them well. Help their teachers see their needs and fulfill them, while helping each fifth grader welcome their instruction and heed what they learn of you. Open the heart and mind of every fifth grader to your word and to the lessons they need to learn to do well in the world and better in your kingdom. Make every fifth grader a lifelong citizen of your kingdom that each of them may know your salvation and have eternal life. Protect every fifth grader against the wiles of the evil one and against their own fleshly desires, so that they may be holy and righteous in your sight. Help every fifth grader to show compassion for one another. Let no unholy word escape their mouths, and instead help them to praise you. In Jesus' name. Amen.

January 30: Aides. Lord God, you have blessed the school with skilled and dedicated classroom aides. They have given their time and service to the school so that the school may effectively pursue its mission to instruct students in your way to serve you. The aides of the school make such a difference in the lives and studies of students that we pray that you will help them know their value to the school.

Make the aides sensitive, supportive, encouraging, wise, and diligent in their instruction and care for the students. Keep the school's aides safe and well, while also protecting their families. Let the aides find rewards both here and in heaven. Help the teachers and administrators to value and encourage the school's aides, recognizing and respecting their contributions to student learning. Help the school recruit, train, and retain skilled and dedicated aides to serve the students. In Jesus' name we pray. Amen.

January 31: Conscience. Father God, give the students of the school your conscience. Help them to learn that they have your Spirit as their guide, to tell them the difference between right and wrong, good and evil, your way and the world's way. Help the teachers to instruct the students in ways that amplify and confirm their conscience, so that they see what you desire and what you despise, and so that they choose your will and not their own or the ways of the world. Raise the conscience of every student who enters the school, so that they desire to obey your commands. Strengthen the conscience of students, so that they will see their adversary's temptations and avoid them. We pray that they flourish under your rule rather than submit to their adversary's deceptions, in violation of their conscience. Make the conscience of every student strong, and strengthen their will to do as you desire. We pray in Jesus' name. Amen.

February 1: Listening. Lord and Savior, we pray today that the students of the school become good listeners, that they listen to your word, listen to their conscience, listen to their teachers, and listen to your Spirit. Help students to quiet their souls, quiet their mouths, and quiet their desires, so that they can listen to and hear your words, their teachers' instruction, and your desires. For we know that through listening, we learn. We know that through listening, we hear. Make the students good listeners of one another, too, that they may learn of their classmates' needs and interests. Make the students good listeners to their parents, so that they may be obedient children in their homes and do as their parents desire. And make the students good listeners for the needs of the community, that they may serve well, showing your love for all. In Jesus' name we pray. Amen.

February 2: Humility. Lord God, you who reign supreme, who are our creator, whom we revere and obey and adore, help the students of the school develop your character, the character of your Son Jesus Christ, of humility. For he was humble in origin and humble in manner and humble in act, yet the King of kings, the Lord of lords, and the creator of all. Help the students to recognize humility as a primary ingredient of their faith, so that they would know that you are their Savior to whom they owe everything. Let them claim no credit that is not their own. Let them give honor where honor is due. And let them not be jealous of the credit and honor others receive, even if they do not receive equal recognition. Help them to know that you see all that they are and do, and that their acclaim is best in you and ultimately in you. Keep them from arrogance and pride. Foster in them the willingness to bow low to you, while accepting the authority of those whom you designate and approve. Thank you, Lord, for your humility and teaching us humility, too. In Jesus' name we pray. Amen.

> **Confession.** You have noticed that many of the daily school prayers begin with confession. Sin is an obstacle to prayer. Confession and repentance remove the sin, opening the door again to fruitful prayer. Confess liberally so that God hears and answers.

February 3: Problem Solving. Lord Almighty, maker of heaven and earth, goodness and light, before whom we kneel in awe, need, and confession, we revere your every aspect, your every desire, your every act. Thank you for creating a cosmos that so gorgeously reflects you, while placing us in relationship to you. Thank you for your desire that we know and pursue you, even as you fully know and passionately pursue us. We desire that the students of the school receive your creative and visionary power, that they learn to see the right questions and pursue your right answers, and that they become problem solvers as you solve every problem. Help them to acquire at the school the knowledge, skills, and values that will enable them to serve themselves, their families, their churches, and their communities as seers and solvers of problems. Help them to receive your word of reason and Spirit of rationality, design, and purpose. Let them be builders in your kingdom. We ask in Jesus' name. Amen.

February 4: Infant Care. God of peace, God of purpose, God of love, we awake each day in awe of your wonders, the greatest of which is the wonder of life in your own image, the wonder of human life, of the unborn and the newborn. Thank you for giving the school its ministry and mission of educating the young after your desires, for service to you in your creation.

We hear of the need of working parents for reliable infant care, reliable daycare, that they may earn incomes to provide for their families while resting assured in the care and upbringing of their children. Make a way for families to care for their own infants, to work within the home both for income and for raising infants and children. Where no such way is possible, help families find reliable infant care outside the home, rewarding infant care workers for their love, sensitivity, and commitment, and drawing together the human and other resources for infant care. If the school is to have a greater role in providing infant care and daycare, then show the board, leader, and staff the way, opening doors to facilities, personnel, programs, and passions to care for these precious young. We ask in Jesus' name. Amen.

February 5: Schedules. Father God, you to whom we entrust all things, even our own lives and the lives and welfare of our children, much as you entrusted your own

Son Jesus Christ to us, giving us his life, taking from him his life that his sacrifice would redeem us and his resurrection would restore and transform us, we give you our entire selves in praise. The school has its own daily and weekly schedule, differing from other schools. Help the school's leader and board discern the best schedule, one that will bring the school community together in unity around you and commitment to learning about you and how you work in the world. Help the families adjust to the school's schedule, finding the transportation and flexibility they need to have their children at school on time and cared for when not at school. Don't let the schedule interfere with your desire for all children to learn of you. We ask in Jesus' name. Amen.

> **Address.** When you pray your daily school prayers, keep in mind that you are not so much addressing God as allowing God to address you. If your prayer is true and holy and right, then the Holy Spirit is already at work within you, forming your thoughts, words, and desires. Your prayers may not be calling out to the Father but instead the Father calling out to you.

February 6: Professional Development. Dear Father, you know the skilled and dedicated staff members of the school who have committed their days and careers to educating your children for service to you in your creation. You know their talents, ambitions, weaknesses, and strengths. You are still at work in each one of them, equipping them with the discernment, insight, sensitivity, judgment, and skills to help the school's students learn. We ask that you continue their professional and spiritual development, even as they teach the students of the school. Help the board and leader provide for their continued development, that they would grow in their effective witness to you. Bring to the school the professional-development resources necessary to refine the staff's knowledge and skills, increasing their effectiveness in pursuing the school's mission to educate minds and shape hearts for service to you. In Jesus' name we pray. Amen.

February 7: City Relationship. Heavenly Father, we thank you for sending us your Son Jesus Christ and for having him accomplish the work that you could then send us your Holy Spirit. We ask that you help the school share the good news of your Son Jesus Christ with the local community in our city, town, or village, so that the life and light and goodness of your Son Jesus Christ would shine through the school and across the community. Help the school's leader, staff members, families, students, volunteers, and board represent you well when interacting with city leaders and residents. Give city leaders, including the city Council and its planning commission, department of public safety, department of public works, and other agencies and officials a heart for the school, an understanding of how it serves the city well, and how the school pursues educating its students to serve you well, thus serving the city well, too. In Jesus Christ's name we pray. Amen.

February 8: Neighbors. Father God, our Savior, our Lord, we know you as the God beyond time and space, above and beyond your creation, yet intimately involved in your creation, especially with us. We thank you for sharing the life and sacrifice of your Son Jesus Christ with us, through whom we know you, approach you, and receive

your mercy. We pray today for the neighbors of the school, the homeowners, renters, and residents whose properties border the school and who share in the daily rhythms of the neighborhood. We pray that you would bless them with your word, presence, and salvation, that they would know you and look to you, and that we would, too. Forgive us our offenses against our neighbors, and help us to forgive them. Make the school a good neighbor, showing the school community how it can serve and encourage those who live, work, and play alongside us. And give the school favor among its neighbors, that the neighbors would support the school before city officials for services and accommodations the school requests in furthering its mission. We have prayed these things today in the name of our Lord Jesus Christ. Amen.

February 9: Discussion. Father, Son, and Spirit, our triune and holy God, we revere you this day and every day, looking to you as our light and life, our creator and the author of all good we do and we receive. Thank you for the revelation of your Son Jesus Christ among us. Help us to share that revelation broadly and lovingly as you would have us do. We pray today that you would help us discuss among board members, staff members, families, students, and volunteers, civilly, sensitively, generously, and in recognition of the inherent value and Christ-like image of each other, issues important to the school and your will for the school. Give us each a listening ear and soft and forgiving heart for others, as others share their insights, experiences, and commitments, and what they hear from you. Give us soft and clear voices as we speak what we each hear from you and see in you. Forgive us when we offend others in discussion, as we forgive others who offend us. And help us to reach accord whenever we disagree with others as to what we believe to be your will, so that we may move forward in unity as you would have us do.

February 10: Ascent. Heavenly Father, on whom we depend for life, meaning, purpose, breath, hope, and eternity, thank you for stooping so low as to enter your creation with the design of rescuing us from our own sin and redeeming your creation for the intention you had for it when you brought it about, when you gave it order and design out of the pre-cosmogonic chaos. We pray today for our continued ascent and the ascent of the students, staff, leader, volunteers, parents, and community of the school, nearing you each season, each day, each hour through your immeasurable mercy and grace. Continue to guide us in your way so that we may continue to grow nearer you, receiving your desire, divinity, and eternity in your kingdom. Help the school to educate its students, your children, in the hope of eternity and participation in your kingdom, where we find our redemption and life. In Jesus' name we pray. Amen.

February 11: Father. Father God, our creator and redeemer, we give the day to you, to think of your goodness, your light, your life, and your glory. We thank you for making the world, for providing for us within the world, and for redeeming us out of the world. We ask today that every student of the school would know you, seek you, and know that you seek them for their good and glory. Call each student to you, helping them to hear you, see you, and feel your embrace, so that they will learn to trust you, depend on you, rely on you, and look to you for everything. Help them to move toward and into your kingdom, to participate as builders of that kingdom, and to take their rightful places as rulers in your kingdom, under your authority and in your mercy and grace. We thank you for being the Father of your only begotten Son Jesus Christ, for bringing him into the world to show yourself to us in human and divine person, as our Savior and as our model and guide, even as our brother and friend. In Jesus' name we pray. Amen.

February 12: Health. God Almighty, we pray today for the health of the students, parents, staff members, leaders, and volunteers of the school. You have given us life and purpose. Now give us good physical and mental health to carry out your desire. Let every student come to school rested and ready to learn about you and your design for them in your good world. Let every student remain healthy through the school day and afterward at home. Help every staff member to recover from disease and injury, and to regain the strength and vitality they need to do your will. Help every volunteer find the physical strength and emotional resources to do as you desire for the school and its students and families. Help the parents find the energy and health to care for their children and to provide for their family so that they may enjoy the benefits of their children learning at the school about you. And give the school's leader the good health and vitality to continue to serve the school. These things we ask in the name of your Son Jesus Christ. Amen.

Purity. If sin is an obstacle to fruitful prayer, then purity can be a door through which prayer rushes. But who is pure? For that reason, we pray in Jesus' name, under his blood, in his authority. We also do well when we enlist in corporate prayer others who value and protect their purity under Jesus' blood. The prayers of the righteous are effective. Stay pure, enlist prayer from the pure, and pray in the name of Jesus.

February 13: Graduates. Father God, creator of heaven and earth, source of all goodness and love, we worship you today with the desire you have given us for you. We fill our hunger not with the desires of the flesh but the call of our spirits to have you, to know you, and to embrace you and have you embrace us. We thank you for the graduates of the school, how they have gone into the world to represent you, to serve you, to share your love and care with those most needful, and to tell others of you. We ask that you bless every graduate of the school, that you secure them in faith, that you remind them today and each day that they walk with you. Protect them from harm, protect their families, and keep them close to you. Give them strong and sound relationships, healthy and saved children and grandchildren, and the things that they need so as not to turn from you. Keep them in your shelter and heart until they join you in your kingdom. In Jesus' name we pray. Amen.

February 14: Vocation. God Almighty, you whom we know also as Wonderful Counselor and Prince of Peace, we have greater need of you every day. Continue to show us our need so that we may turn more to you, grow more in you, and lose the things we must lose not to offend you. We pray

today that you call the students of the school into their vocations, that you help each student to see what they have the capacity, interest, reach, and call to do for you in your creation. Bring to the minds of the teachers of the school the professionals, tradespersons, homemakers, and others who serve you, so that the teachers can help the students see examples of how they, too, can serve you with whatever talents you have blessed them. Give the students the desire, will, and motivation to pursue vocations that represent you well to others, in healing, making, growing, managing, administering, leading, creating, and the other things you do and have your people do for you. In Jesus' name we pray. Amen.

February 15: Building Design. Father God, you who make us stand back in wonder at who you are and what you do, we credit, honor, and praise you for all creation, for all goodness, for all love, for all glory. We know that we are so much less than you and so wholly in need of you. Forgive us when we claim credit that is yours and forget to whom we owe all things, none other than you. You know that we have the blessing of looking forward to new plans for the expansion of the school. You know the hours and days we have spent with skilled designers to plan an expansion that honors you and serves you, through the educational mission you have given the school. Help the design team develop the best plans. Help us to communicate the needs of the school. Bring us together around a plan that will serve the school well. Let each member of the design team exercise their best skills for you, while knowing the gratitude of the school. And then see that the plan comes to fruition in an expanded school that can serve more of your children. We pray in the name of Jesus Christ. Amen.

February 16: Space. Father of glory, Father of lights, Father of life, we thank you for regarding the school as one of your own, for blessing it with a long history and rich legacy of graduates, and for growing it over the years and into the present season. We credit your Spirit with giving parents the heart for Christian education, to send their students to the school. We thank you for growing the school. The school faces space needs for the Fall, especially if it loses a classroom to new construction. Help the school's board, leader, and staff members discern the best solution to fill those space needs so that the school doesn't have to turn away students. Help the school serve every family wishing to send their students to the school. Show us the space you would have us use, and then give the school the resources to improve the space for the students to occupy next Fall. You have everything under control. All is in your hands, we trust. Just let us do as you will. We pray in the name of our Lord Jesus Christ. Amen.

February 17: Anxiety. Heavenly Father, maker of heaven and earth, we worship you today and every day, knowing that all we have is in you. Continue to turn our hearts toward you and your heaven, that we may join you in your kingdom. Give us the long view of you. Indeed, we ask today that you would relieve the students of the school of anxiety, that their hearts would no longer suffer the burden of unreasonable fears, that they would no longer miss out on education, relationships, and the other good things the school has to offer them because of how anxious they feel. You know how students are suffering because of being anxious over things they need to face for their own growth, whether joining their classmates or taking tests or just making their way through the day. Show students the things they can and cannot control, and help them to look past the things they cannot control. Lift the spirits of every student of the school. Guard the heart of every student of the school. Give the students courage and strength to persevere in the face of anxious feelings. Declare the school free of anxiety, making it a safe zone for students to experience the lightness and liberty they have in you. In Jesus' name we pray. Amen.

Humility. God's word makes clear that he listens to the prayer of the humble. The humble are those who confess their sins and pray for his mercy rather than those who point to the sins of others and pray for what they mistakenly believe they deserve. Pray your daily school prayers humbly, not arrogantly.

February 18: Board Unity. Father God, our Savior, you who provide and bless and guide and instruct and encourage and comfort, we embrace you and revere you and worship you. Forgive us our sins, our short-sightedness, our selfishness, and our lack of trust. We pray today that you would continue to guide and inform and instruct the school board with your discernment and desires, that we would listen for you, hear you, and follow you in all you wish from us and for us. Thank you for the skills, character, and commitment of the board members and especially for their devotion to you. Keep us unified in pursuit of the school's mission to draw its students ever nearer to you. Let us disagree agreeably, civilly, respectfully, so that we can share what we each hear from you, and let us listen to one another, incorporate one another's discernment, and move forward together in pursuit of your desires for the school. We pray in the name of our Lord and Savior Jesus Christ. Amen.

February 19: Unity. Dear Father, we come before you today with the desire that the school community would draw together in unity under your Holy Spirit, as a devoted part of the body of Christ, all members respecting and valuing one another, with our disagreements quickly set aside in favor of joining with one another in pursuit of you. Unify the students in their commitment to you, the staff members in their devotion to you, the volunteers in their desire for you, and the board and leader in their passion for doing your will. Let every guest who enters the school see the unity we have in Jesus Christ, how Christ resolves differences into joy in worshiping and serving with brothers and sisters in the faith. Thank you for giving us the best of all things around which to unify, and that is our trust in you as the one great God, sovereign over all, for our eternal good. In Jesus' name we pray. Amen.

February 20: Deepening. Holy Father, to whom we owe our everything, from our existence to our provision to our purpose, we celebrate you, commit to you, devote ourselves to you, and give ourselves up to you, with the hope that you will accept us in Jesus Christ your only begotten Son, whose sacrifice was for our sins and redeemed us in a way that we could never redeem ourselves. We pray today that every member of the school community will grow deeper in faith, today and each day forward to the end of the school year and beyond. We want to see your glory, to know your profound purpose and desire for each one of us and for the school community and broader church of Jesus Christ corporately and collectively. Help us to ground our own desires in the deepest desires, purest patterns, and highest principles you have for us, indeed in your commands and way. Help us to find in the depths of your wisdom all we need and the answers to all we ask. In Jesus' name we pray. Amen.

February 21: Pastors. Dear God, the one whom we trust and on whom we rely for everything, indeed for our every breath and certainly for the breath of life that comes with knowing you and your desires and purpose for us, we pray today for the pastors who support the school with their preaching, worship, and service, and with entrusting the children of their church to the school. We pray that you would strengthen each pastor, equip each pastor for your ministry, guard the mental and physical health of each pastor, and unite each pastor with the school in its mission to draw students to you for service in your creation. We pray that you would heal the school's pastors where they need healing, comfort them where they need comfort, and

provide the same for their families and for the members of their congregation. We thank you for each of the school's pastors and pray that they would know how the school loves and values them. In Jesus' name we pray. Amen.

February 22: Time. Father God, forgive us today for how we waste time, spend time on frivolous pursuits, and guard time as if it were our own. You number our days. You grant us each hour. We want to spend time, use time, treat time in ways that you would have us do. Give the students of the school the time they need for effective studies, reflection, rest, recovery, and creative play, too. Give the staff members time for instruction, preparation, rest, recovery, healing, and inspiration, too. Give the school leader the time to attend to all duties and responsibilities, while also envisioning what you desire for the school and doing all those things that would carry out your desire. Give the board members the time to commit to the school, to serve the school, and to hear your desires for governing the school toward the future you have for the school. Slow down time when we need time to be slow, and speed up time when we need it to pass quickly. Help us to be grateful for the time you give us, to be good stewards of that time, and use the time to draw closer to you. In Jesus' name we pray. Amen.

February 23: Graduation. God our Father, on whom we depend and whom we worship, thank you for bringing the eighth graders of the school to the staff and school community, for the devotion and trust of their parents, and the perseverance they have shown through the curriculum. We celebrate their coming graduation, thanking you for drawing them closer to you through the community of the school, blessed by your Holy Spirit. Encourage the graduates that they have accomplished something dear to you, that they would commit their studies to knowing you and preparing to serve you. Help them to celebrate their accomplishment with joy and gratitude. Help the school to celebrate with them. Let each of them retain the faith with which you have blessed and equipped them, and help them to encourage one another for the rest of this year and on into the future, as classmates forever. In Jesus' name we pray. Amen.

> **Primacy.** When we pray our daily school prayers, we should put God first. Remember, to the degree our prayers are authentic, the Holy Spirit is already speaking those prayers to us. Our prayer should thus be about him, his actions already at work in our soul, rather than so much about us. Humble, effective prayer makes God primary, just as he is, infinitely greater in respect to us, but also infinitely caring for us.

February 24: First Responders. God Almighty, maker of heaven and earth, provider and comforter, Savior and friend, we trust you, depend on you, rely on you, and need you, every day, every hour, with every breath. Hear our prayers today, giving us the pure and repentant heart that you love, and then answer our prayers out of your mercy and grace. We pray today for the first responders serving the school and the surrounding community. We pray that you would give the police officers, firefighters, and medical personnel the courage, strength, health, and discipline to protect the school and surrounding community in all emergency needs, whether security threats or threats from artificial or natural disasters. Make them swift, sure, and effective in their actions, while keeping them safe and from suffering injury or other harm. Reward and encourage them for their service, and equip them with all they need. Thank you for the school's first responders. In the name of Jesus Christ our Lord we pray. Amen.

February 25: Board Recruiting. Father God, whom we worship and celebrate and obey, whose grace encourages us, whose mercy forgives us, and who provides all we need, help us this day to bring to the board of the school members who share the mission you have given the school, to educate minds and shape hearts for service to you in your creation. Help the board to identify members who have the

skills and experience the board needs, the devotion to you the school must maintain, and the ear for your guidance, so that the school may flourish in bringing its students nearer to you. Help the candidates to search their hearts for the willingness to serve and the devotion to you that will hearten the board and help to govern the school. Let the board exercise your wisdom in discerning the candidates to encourage and welcome to the board, for the board is your body, your tool, submitted wholly to you. In Jesus' name we pray. Amen.

February 26: Conviction. Heavenly Father, our shepherd, our protector, our guide, we thank you for giving the founders of the school the vision to form it and guide it through its early years. We thank you for equipping the school, giving it a home and staff and the enrollment to carry out its vital mission of educating your young, those students whose parents have devoted them to you. We thank you for entrusting the school to the current board and leader. We accept that role and responsibility, humbly, knowing that we need your word, your guidance, and the conviction that we must boldly follow you when the world would lead us away from you. Help us to discern where we must act courageously, transparently, and with conviction in holding onto you, obeying and sharing your word even when and especially when others oppose it. Help us to discern with conviction where you would have us stand firm and openly on your truth. We pray in the name of Jesus our Lord. Amen.

February 27: Consent. Dear God, our Father, we thank you for the parents who have entrusted the education of their children to the school. We pray today that they would continue in their trust, that they would consent that the school educate their children consistent with its biblical stance and faith commitment as the school expresses. Help parents to understand the school's commitment, respect that commitment, and carry it out in their relationship with the school, supporting the staff and volunteers and leader, in the education of their children in the tenets of the faith. Let the parents of the school's students join heartily and joyfully with the school in that commitment to the education of their children in your word, your way, your righteousness. Let the bond of trust grow, and let parents express it in ways that encourage the staff to teach their children your truth with passion and devotion. And help the school's leader determine how best to gain that hearty consent from parents that the school may unify around its distinctive mission, so apart from the world's ways. In the name of our Lord and Savior Jesus Christ we pray. Amen.

February 28: Partner Schools. Heavenly Father, you have given the school partner schools, whose leaders and staff encourage and inform the school. Help us to determine how to partner with other Christian schools in the area that share in the school's mission. Help the staff to find ways to draw on the insights and experiences of the staff at those partner schools. Help the school's leader to draw on the insights and experiences of the leaders of those other schools. And if you determine that the school should find other ways to connect with partner schools, then guide the leader and board toward those partnerships. We recognize that we share the opportunity and responsibility to educate young minds and shape young hearts for service to you in your creation. Help us identify, respect, and support those other partner schools. Guide the school's leader and the school's board if you desire the school to form new partnerships with other area Christian schools. We entrust this issue and its opportunities to your guidance. In the name of our Lord Jesus Christ we pray. Amen.

> **Reality.** Prayer has a way of showing us what is real. We spend so much of our day seeing through lenses of unreality, thinking in the world's ways rather than in the way that God designed and reveals his creation. Prayer brings us back to God's authentic way of seeing his creation rather than the distorted ways the world encourages us to view it. Treasure your daily school prayer.

February 29: Learning. Father God, in whom we trust for all things, including how to learn about you and your desires, your instructions and commands, your grace and mercy, and your love and sacrifice in your Son Jesus Christ, we pray today that you would make us a community of learners, that the students of the school would learn of you and your way, that they would become learners, skilled at learning including identifying the things they should seek after and learn about, especially your word and will, that they may serve you. Help the staff to discern how to encourage students to learn, take responsibility for their learning, and develop the meta cognitive skills to learn. Help the staff to become better learners themselves, even as they help students to learn. Make the school a community of growth, exploration, inspiration, and learning, all of your righteous way. We desire to learn of you, learn from you, and learn what you would have us do in your creation to dwell richly within your kingdom. In the name of our Lord Jesus Christ we pray. Amen.

March 1: Disabilities. Dear God, our Father, you who are our all, our everything, in whom we live and dwell and have our being, we pray today for the students with disabilities, for students who need special instruction, support, and guidance, for students whose capacities differ, who need remediation and modified services and special resources. We pray that you would equip the school and its staff to provide for the needs of students with disabilities and that

you would equip those students with the capacities you know they will need in life to carry out your will. We recognize that each student is unique and individual, each made in your image, and that the school must help each student learn within their capacity and preparedness to do so. Make students able, reduce and eliminate disabilities, and encourage parents and staff members and volunteers to stand alongside students who wish to overcome and eliminate their disabilities, while drawing richly on their abilities. Give the school community a heart for students whose needs differ, while helping all students reach their capacities. In Jesus' name we pray. Amen.

March 2: Retired Staff. Father God, Holy One, our redeemer and provider, who have your Son Jesus Christ for us, we thank you for the service of the teachers and aides and other staff members of the school who have given their careers to the school and are retiring soon or have retired. Strengthen those retiring or retired staff members for their remaining ministry. Help them find new ministries after your desire. Keep them in good health so that they may enjoy their remaining years in retirement. Keep them encouraged over their long ministry for the school, and help the school welcome them back and recognize them for their service. Do not let them believe their work was in vain. Show them the fruits of their work so that they may receive your encouragement and so that they may encourage the current staff in their labors and ministry. Provide for retiring and retired staff in their financial and material needs, but especially in their spiritual needs, so that they may continue to walk closely with you, growing even closer to you. And let the school then find other staff to fulfill the retiring and retired staff members' roles with the same dedication, skill, and devotion. In Jesus' name we pray. Amen.

March 3: Parents. Holy Father, God Almighty, protector, comforter, and provider, we worship, adore, and praise you. We bow down to you, give our all to you, and submit our hopes and desires to you. We thank you for your mercy and grace, for giving us your Son as redemption for our corruption and wrongs. Today we ask that you bless, protect, guide, and encourage the parents of the school, those faithful servants of yours who send their children to the school trusting that they will learn more of you and prepare themselves for serving you as their parents already do. We ask that you equip and provide for the parents in all their challenges to do right by their children and do right by you. We ask that you give the parents the sense of satisfaction and assurance of knowing that they are doing your will for their children, as they give their children to you. Help the school to serve you and the parents of the school's students well. We thank you for the parents of the school's students. In Jesus' name we pray. Amen.

March 4: Marriages. Dear Father, you who are our Savior and Provider, we thank you for the many marriages we see at work so fruitfully in the school, including the marriages of the parents of the school's students, the marriages of the staff members, the marriages of the volunteers and grandparents, and other marriages we see blessing the school. Within those marriages, we see the trust, care, love, and loyalty, and the mercy, grace, and forgiveness you offer us and ask of us for you and for one another. Bless the marriages of the school, and bless the school through those marriages. Let the students of the school grow up to be fruitful and loving spouses in trusting and loyal marriages that bring many children into your world to love and receive you. In Jesus' holy name we pray. Amen.

> **Time.** We should make time for our daily school prayers. Time, in the discipline to take a moment, minute, or hour to pray, may be prayer's single most important ingredient. Your time may be when waking up, at the noon hour, or in the quiet of day's end. Whatever your rhythm may be, take the time to pray.

March 5: Commitment. Heavenly Father, Prince of Peace, we pray today that you would give every member of the school community the strongest sense of commitment to your word, your way, your truth, and your light. Do not let the board, the school leader, the school's staff members, the parents of the school's students, nor the students themselves waver in their commitment to you. Do not let us assume the ways of the world, rejecting your truths for the lies the world offers. Instead, hold us to the faith, keep us true to the convictions you would have us receive in your word and way. Reveal to us where we have erred or are turning away from you. Let us adhere to your doctrine, embrace your character, and reflect your will in all we do, no matter the cost, even as we seek to be peacemakers and peacekeepers in all we do. In Jesus' name we pray. Amen.

March 6: Great-Grandparents. Dear God, our Father and Savior, we are in awe of your mercy in giving your Son Jesus Christ for us, for our sins, to redeem us and bring us back to you. We are in awe of your creation and of your goodness and beauty reflected in your grand design for all we see and know. We thank you for the precious legacy of the school you have entrusted to us, for the generations of families who have permitted the school to educate their

children. We thank you especially today for the school's great-grandparents, for the living and departed members of the school community who have seen not just their children enter the school or their grandchildren but also their great-grandchildren, a fourth generation learning about you at the school. We pray for the health, comfort, faith, and encouragement of the school's great-grandparents, that you would bless them to the end of their earthly days and let them feel the school's gratitude, too. In the name of our Lord and Savior Jesus Christ we pray. Amen.

March 7: Influenza. Father God, our healer and comforter, we pray today that you would guard the school's students, staff, leader, and community from the common and uncommon influenza that make attending, learning, teaching, and serving so difficult. We thank you for healing those who have suffered or are suffering from the flu, and we ask that you continue to do so. Let us learn more of you through our suffering the flu and other illnesses and hardships, for we know that you suffered far greater in your love for us. Let us care for one another when others are sick, even as we seek and accept the care of others when we are sick, too. Strengthen those who must take on extra duties and roles to cover tasks usually completed by those who are out sick. And restore the school community to good health, confident in your care and seeking to draw closer to you. We pray in Jesus' name. Amen.

March 8: Will. Heavenly Father, Father of Lights, you who are all goodness and love, without whom we would suffer entirely in the dark, we recognize today that we have no request of you, no prayer for you, greater than that your will be done. We want your will accomplished with the school, with every student who enters and leaves its doors, with every parent alike, and with the leader, board, staff, and volunteers of the school, too. We pray that your desire be precisely and entirely what occurs within the school's walls, on its playgrounds and parking lots, and in the surrounding community, even in the homes of every student, staff member, and volunteer of the school. Father, your will, not our will, be done. Father, your desire, not our desire, be at the forefront of all we seek and do. Father, your kingdom come, on earth as it is in heaven. In Jesus' name we pray. Amen.

March 9: Middle School. Father God, whose desires are our own, we pray today for the school's middle school, for the students of the middle school, for the families who have middle-school students, and for the staff and volunteers of the middle school. Keep the middle school's spirit your righteous Holy Spirit. Keep the middle school's culture your Christian culture, in the Spirit of your loving and sacrificial and courageous and gentle Son. Keep the middle school strong, like your Son is strong. Keep the middle school pure, like your Son Jesus is pure. Keep the middle school vital, like your Holy Spirit energizes and vitalizes. Protect the middle school, as you protect and uplift the believer and the righteous. And bless the middle school so that it stands as a beacon to your love. In the name of our Lord and Savior Jesus Christ. Amen.

March 10: Stewardship. Dear heavenly Father, our righteousness, our hope, and our guide, you have left the board of the school with a treasured history, legacy, and mission. Help us to be good stewards of what you have given us to govern, to foster, to preserve, and to promote in your way and your will. Don't let us squander anything of what the past has sacrificed for the present and future. Guide us to preserve the school's resources and mission for future students and generations of students, so that the school would be in your kingdom and of your kingdom, teaching all to serve your desires. Make us fit for the decisions and insights and courage and commitment that governing the school may require. Show us your vision. Open doors through which you wish us to walk, and close doors you would have us ignore. Don't let us be proud or thoughtless or misguided or reckless but instead listening and adhering to you. Guard us with your Spirit. Open our eyes to your will. In the name of Jesus Christ our Lord we pray. Amen.

Priority. Your daily school prayer helps you keep your priorities straight. God first, and God's desires. Then other important things, in their order of priority. Life is a lot about being able to keep things in their order of priority. Many things are important but some things more than others. Your daily school prayer helps keep your priorities straight.

March 11: Process. Father God, you who are our glory and aim, thank you for your mercy toward us, for blessing us with the governance of the school and for giving us the insight and guidance we need to undertake that governance well, after your will and righteousness. Forgive us when we have not listened to your word and discerned your will, when we have shortchanged the process you would have us follow to hear you and hear your witnesses, to see you and see your actions among us. Help us to follow the steps you would have us follow, to listen to the constituents to whom you would have us listen, to hear the voices you would have us hear, and to be both patient and prompt, cautious and courageous, flexible and persevering. Lead the board's process in all things. We give our will to you. In the name of our Lord and Savior Jesus Christ we pray. Amen.

March 12: Sister Schools. Father of lights, Father of glory, Father of all goodness, thank you for sharing the life of your Son Jesus Christ, for showing such unfathomable mercy out of your loving kindness. May we bless you back today and each day, following your Spirit, doing your will, and pursuing your kingdom. We pray today for our sister schools in Christian education, for the local schools who lift you up to their students, who train their students in the way of the good Lord, sharing richly the good news of Jesus Christ. We ask that you bless and protect those schools, in their mission, finance, staffing, leadership, governance, safety, security, and spirit. Keep their enrollment strong, grow their reach, strengthen their staff, and bless their students and their families. Let them continue their good work, sharing your word and spreading the good news of your Son. We pray in his glorious name. Amen.

March 13: Reputation. God Almighty, Lord of heaven and earth, we come to you without complaint, without merit, without claim, and instead humbly, undeserving, and in need. We recognize your mercy and grace, and we relish it, depending on it fully, without taking advantage.

Our prayer today is for the reputation of the school, that the school would stand as a beacon of light to the community, with a good reputation. We ask that you protect the school against accusers, slanderers, and liars who would diminish the school's reputation to harm its students, staff, and mission. We ask that you open the hearts and minds of all to the good that the school does by adhering to your word and pursuing your desires. We further ask that you give every student, family, staff member, and volunteer of the school the good credit in the eyes of others that they earn and deserve, so that we may all promote the school's mission to turn students and others to you. We pray in the name of our incomparable Lord Jesus Christ. Amen.

March 14: Lord. Father God, we pray today that you would teach us what it means for you to be our Lord. We speak of you as Lord, yet we want to act with you as Lord and be in relationship to you with you as our Lord. Help the students, families, staff, leader, board, and volunteers of the school to know you as Lord, treat you as Lord, and relate to you as Lord. Give us the spirit of submission to your will, the desire to do your will, and the willingness to raise you up above us in all we do. Help us to stand under your banner as Lord and not under the banner of your adversary. Give us the righteousness that comes with our treating you rightfully as our Lord. Let your Spirit inform our consciences when we do not treat you as Lord so that we may confess, repent, and seek and exalt you once again as Lord. Be our Lord. We pray in the name of our Lord Jesus Christ. Amen.

March 15: Repentance. Dear Heavenly Father, our holy God, we ask your forgiveness in the name and under the blood of your Son Jesus Christ. We pray today that you give the school and its students, families, staff, leader, board, and volunteers your Holy Spirit of repentance, that we would see our sin, confess our sin, and turn away from sin. Help us to have the will and desire to stop violating your commands and start obeying as the righteous should, as the followers of your Son should. Give us a spirit of submission including especially the desire to obey your commands, meet your standards, pursue your principles, and follow your patterns and desires. Help us to rid our lives and relationships and routes of the patterns of corruption. Give us a clean life and clean spirit after your Holy Spirit. Wash us of all wrong, and then fill us with a life of righteousness so that we have no desire to do other than as you will. We ask in the name of our Savior Jesus. Amen.

March 16: Lent. Father God, in your righteousness, holiness, and mercy, we approach you today thinking of this period of Lent, as we prepare to celebrate the finished work of your Son on the cross, his resurrection, and our redemption under his blood and risen self. Give us the spirit of preparation, of prayer, fasting, and giving of alms. Let us see our own path to the cross, carrying our own crosses as your Son said we must in honor and memory of his own cross borne so perfectly and painfully for us. Give us your spirit of humility, of sacrifice, of the denial of our flesh, as your Son denied his flesh to do your will on the cross. In the spirit of Lent we find our peace, satisfaction, and path through this blessed but also difficult life ministering after your will on earth before our own redemption. Pour out your spirit of sacrifice and peace in suffering, as we prepare for Holy Week and the great celebration of your Son's resurrection on the Lord's Day. Let the school community look forward to that glorious day in which we see our salvation anew. In the name of Jesus Christ, we pray. Amen.

March 17: Courage. Dear Heavenly Father, our glory whom we desire to serve and bless, we pray today that you would give every student, staff member, leader, and volunteer of the school community your courage, the courage of your Son Jesus Christ to proceed in your will and righteousness, in the path that you desire. Make the

students and staff members not just strong but willing to use the strength with which you bless them to stand for you in all that you ask of them. Help the board members do the same, discerning and doing your will with courage. Help us each to see and overcome our fears, to stand against fear, to follow your word and commands, and to pursue the opportunities you present to us with the passion that you desire. In the name of Jesus Christ our Lord we pray. Amen.

March 18: Preparation. Father God, our hope and rescuer, our Savior and friend, our Father and the Son whom we know and pursue, we thank you for your glory, your presence, your comfort, and your strength. Help the school community to prepare for you what you will bring to us, both gifts and challenges. Help us to maintain our discipline, build our resolve, and adopt the attitude of constantly striving after your will, comforted and encouraged by knowing that you have already arranged and prepared to accomplish what you desire from us. Show us what to do to prepare to do your will. Show us where we need to add or subtract, increase or decrease, store up or expend. Show us the steps for preparation, and give us the discipline and will to prepare. And give us a glimpse of what you have for us to undertake, so that we may know how to prepare. In the name of our Lord and Savior Jesus Christ we pray. Amen.

> **Hierarchy.** God's creation is hierarchical. Things have their place in relationship to one another. The lower pursues and reflects the higher, with God the highest. Your daily school prayer helps you recognize and respect God's hierarchical design, promoting a fruitful and ordered liberty within that design.

March 19: Insight. God Almighty, wonderful Father, Prince of Peace, we have such limited vision, so little knowledge of what was, what is, and what is to come. You have our future in your hands, and we trust that you are the best one and only one to make the right decisions for us, to provide for us as we need, and to guide us into your kingdom along your path of righteousness. We pray today that you would give each member of the school community the insight we need to live according to your will and way, with your blessing, in honor to you. Show us what we need to see about our past, our present, and our future to make decisions and judgments informed by you rather than by our biases and prejudices, our limited and corrupted sight. Give us the clarity, hope, and vision that comes with knowing your truth. Let us follow a process of prayer, submission, dedication, devotion, and reflection that leads us to the insights you would have us reach to proceed as you would have us do. Clear our spirits and minds to see your way. Reveal yourself and your movement to us. Give us fresh and enduring insights. We ask these things in the name of our Lord Jesus Christ. Amen.

March 20: Relationship. Heavenly Father, our desire at the school is that every student would know you, have a place in their heart in which they find your Son Jesus Christ, and hear your word for their lives so that they can serve you. We pray today that you would bless every student of the school with a warm, deep, and secure relationship with your Son Jesus Christ, through your Holy Spirit, dwelling richly in their hearts that you have transformed in a new birth for new life and eternal victory. Help the teachers and volunteers and families of the school love and guide and correct and encourage each student to value and embrace their relationship with you and your Son Jesus Christ. Let each student be a witness to their families and others of their relationship with you and your Son Jesus Christ. We ask these things in his very name, our Lord Jesus Christ. Amen.

March 21: Identity. Father God, we pray today that the students of the school would find their identity in you, created in your image, and in their relationship with your Son Jesus Christ. Do not let them seek their identity in the world or in what the world offers them, whether in the desires or accomplishments of the flesh, or the abilities or disabilities that the world says they have, or even in their experiences of hardship, loss, victory, ease, or success. Help them to see that they are your children and that their value, identity, and image come from you and how you think of them, care for them, equip them, and bless and challenge them. Let them find meaning in you, purpose in you, comfort in you, and satisfaction in you. Guard them against depending on the world for their esteem, pride, or self-value. Give them their true image revealed in their relationship with your Son Jesus Christ and all he accomplished on the cross for them. And help the school's teachers to foster in the students that sense of value, worth, and identity in Jesus Christ. In his glorious name we pray. Amen.

March 22: Resurrection. Heavenly Father, we glorify you and bless you, placing you above all else within your creation, knowing that you are the creator of all good. In this time of Lent, we remember all you asked of your Son Jesus Christ and all you gave us when you led him to the cross, and all that he accomplished for us and for your creation when submitting to your will. We pray today that the students of the school will know of your Son's resurrection, that after three days he rose again, ending the hold of death over us and over creation, and bringing us with him into your kingdom. Let every student embrace their own salvation by acknowledging both the crucifixion and resurrection of Jesus Christ, to rescue them from the hold of sin on their lives and the hold of death. May every student of the school receive your salvation to join the heavenly host to glorify you eternally. We thank you for bringing your Son back to life and bringing us to life with him. We pray in the holy name of Jesus Christ the Messiah and our Lord. Amen.

March 23: Administrators. Lord God Almighty, today we pray for the administrators of the school, these mighty souls who take on the school's organization and operation with such verve and vitality, all supplied by you. We thank you for them, for the gifts of memory, devotion, commitment, and consistency with which you have blessed them for service to you through the school's mission. We thank you for their skill, their discernment, their judgment, and the care they exhibit for every student, family, staff member, graduate, and volunteer of the school. We ask that you protect them against the adversary and accuser, that you protect them against illness and injury, and that you bless them with even greater love and energy to carry out their critical mission on behalf of the school's students. We also ask that you help us each to show our appreciation for their dedication to the school, through our own care for them. These things we ask in the name of our Lord Jesus Chris. Amen.

> **Place.** For reliable daily prayer, we generally need to find the right place to pray. Any place of relative solitude may do, such as your bedroom, bathroom, study, or office, or even your barn, work shed, woods, field, truck, or car. Find your best place. Then stick to it. God awaits.

March 24: Core Beliefs. Dear Heavenly Father, Wonderful Counselor, Prince of Peace, we come to you today eager to celebrate Holy Week, culminating in our celebration of the resurrection of your Son Jesus Christ next Sunday. On the eve of Holy Week, we think of the school's core beliefs around the divinity, sonship, ministry, crucifixion, and resurrection of the Messiah Jesus Christ in whom we believe and trust. Help the school's leader and board to identify, declare, and communicate those core beliefs of the faith so that every student, family, staff member, volunteer, and guest of the school would know in whom the school trusts and on whom it depends, and the reason for its confidence in eternal life. Let the school's core beliefs be your word, your will, your revelation, in just the form you would have the school communicate those beliefs. Make our every word faithful to you and helpful to the mission with which you have blessed the school, that every student would have a heart for you and mind for your service. In the name of our Lord Jesus Christ, we pray. Amen.

March 25: Holy Week. Father God, we are here at Palm Sunday, at the beginning of another glorious Holy Week, celebrating your Son Jesus Christ's entry into Jerusalem, soon to take his seat on his throne, the cross, and to conquer death in his resurrection on that incomparable dawn, at the hinge of history. Help us this week to walk with the lightness that the good news of your Son's resurrection should bring, your Son having conquered our eternal enemy to give us eternal life with you. We thank you for the knowledge of heaven, of paradise, and of eternal life, and for your having opened to us the route to our eternal destination with you. We pray today that the school community would find itself enthralled again with the brightness and relief and joy of Holy Week, as you guide us toward the celebration of that great day when your Son walked from the tomb to lead the disciples into their own glory spreading the good news of eternal life. Help us to celebrate appropriately, so that every student may know the joy of life in Jesus Christ. We pray in his name. Amen.

March 26: Clearing the Temple. Dear Heavenly Father, on this Monday of Holy Week, we remember how your Son Jesus Christ cleared your great Temple courtyards of the money changers. We pray today that you would help us to clear our temple of our money changers, of the empty and

even dishonest transactions that we substitute for your holiness, your proximity, your relationship. Help every member of the school community to put aside all dishonesty, all advantage, all gain-seeking, and all unnecessary and unfair transactions, in favor of your presence, your relationship, and your holiness. Do not let us make our faith in you and our holy spaces into dens of robbers, but instead keep our persons and prayers free of unholiness, keep us and our prayers pure. Change our hard hearts into hearts for you, having received your Holy Spirit, nurturing the sensitivity and purity you would have us show. In Jesus' glorious name we pray. Amen.

March 27: Poise. Father God, our Savior and judge and friend, we pray today that you would bless every member of the school community with the poise of which your holy word speaks, that we would each be moved but not shaken, stirred but not confused, impassioned but not out of balance. Let us not prattle on but instead hold our peace to speak only your word and only when encouraging to others. Help us to maintain an equilibrium through the chaotic waters of the world, through the challenges and mysteries of life. Let you be our balance beam, our rock and stabilizer. Give every student of the school the equanimity that comes with knowing the truth, the good news, and the incomparable Lord Jesus Christ. Let others marvel at how the students carry on untroubled by the annoyances and challenges of life, and instead resolute in the knowledge of their salvation and their blessing under your rule. We pray in the name of Jesus Christ our Lord. Amen.

March 28: Maundy Thursday. God our Father, we celebrate Maundy Thursday, remembering how your Son Jesus Christ shared a last supper with his disciples, revealing his glory more fully, revealing himself as your Son more completely. We thank you for the biblical record of that last supper, for the prayer your Son made to you on the disciples' behalf and by extension on our behalf, a prayer you answered completely in the crucifixion and resurrection of your Son, and your blessing us with your Holy Spirit and your eternal kingdom. We treasure the biblical account of your Son's communion with you and his disciples at that last supper, continuing that ritualistic, liturgical communion tradition, receiving your Son's broken body and poured-out blood as our redemption. Reveal all that you have for us to know and do and follow from the last supper, communion, and the good news that followed of your Son's resurrection from the dead. Let every student and family of the school remember the last supper and celebrate communion with you. We pray in our Lord Jesus Christ's name. Amen.

March 29: Good Friday. Heavenly Father, we shudder to think of all that you did when you gave your Son Jesus Christ over to the world, so that the world could crucify him as a criminal, when he was entirely unworthy of condemnation and instead the good and perfect creator, healer, and ruler of the world. But we know on this Good Friday that out of his suffering, blood, and death you revealed the greatest of all achievements, the conquering of pain, sin, and death, and to rescue humankind and

redeem all creation from sin and death, for eternal life with you. Help us on this Good Friday to know what your plan cost you and your Son Jesus Christ, and how dearly we should hold our salvation in your Son, knowing that cost. Let us never forget that as little or much as we may give to you, you have given infinitely more in giving us your Son's own life. Help the students and families of the school celebrate Good Friday appropriately, knowing this most-difficult stage in your grand narrative, your holy arc for the world, out of which you redeem and embrace us, drawing us out of our own sin and death, back to your eternal embrace. In Jesus' name we pray. Amen.

March 30: Burial. Dear God our Father, we pray remembering your Son's burial, the day between his crucifixion and resurrection when he was in the bowels of the earth and all that he accomplished on that sad but also glorious day. Help us to remember what death robs from the living and what descent into the lower reaches means, isolation from you and all that you hold for us and offer to us. Let every student of the school know how Christ's death and burial also buried their sins, when they confess and repent of those sins. Remind us of the faith of Joseph of Arimathea and Nicodemus, caring for the body of Jesus Christ and placing it in the tomb out of which he would rise on the morrow. Let us experience their sadness as a prelude to the joy we experience, in the following morning with the news of the resurrection of Jesus Christ from the dead. We pray in his holy name. Amen.

> **Weakness.** Prayer doesn't depend on power. It may instead depend on our weakness. God perfects his power within our weakness. Thus, don't pray out of your perceived power. Admit your weakness. Rely on God in your daily school prayer.

March 31: Resurrection Day. Father God, we celebrate your risen Son Jesus Christ, who when he walked from the grave brought with him everyone who would recognize and repent of their sin, and believe and trust in his resurrection. Let every student of the school embrace that good news that with the confession of our need for your Son and our belief in his rising from death that we, too, would receive eternal life in which we would know you and know your Son. Help every student and family celebrate your Son's resurrection and the freedom from sin and death that his resurrection accomplished. Let each of us trust in you, receive your Holy Spirit, and walk in righteousness and with the joy of the good news that you conquered sin and death through your Son's sacrifice and resurrection. We need the good news, and we receive and share the good news. May the school community bless you joyfully and generously today and each day in recognition of what you have given us and given the world in your grand redemption. In Jesus' name we pray. Amen.

April 1: Wilderness. Almighty God, our Father, we pray today remembering that you brought the Israelites out of slavery and into the wilderness, and that you also sent your Son Jesus Christ out of his baptism and into the wilderness, so that these journeys would transform the wilderness from a place of danger and destruction to a place of life with you. Feed each student and staff member of the school by the brook in the wilderness. Lead each student through the wilds and into your shelter, protected, redeemed, restored, and freed by you. Let each student experience the wilderness not as a place of danger and confusion but as a place where they meet and come to know and trust you. Be present for them in each wilderness season, in each wilderness event, so that they see and hear you. Strengthen us each through the wilderness, preparing us to enter the promised land of your kingdom. Teach us about the wilderness and the mystery and wild that we see in you. We pray in the name of our Lord Jesus Christ. Amen.

April 2: Ministry. Heavenly Father, we bless and glorify you today, thanking you for revealing yourself in your Son Jesus Christ, our Savior and Lord. We pray that you would give every student of the school a ministry of your word, will, and way, whether that be to teach, witness, heal, protect, parent, produce, administer, or otherwise participate in your kingdom. Give each student the knowledge that they have a role to fulfill for you. Help the school's staff and volunteers to equip each student to serve you in whatever ministry you have for them. Let them become physicians, nurses, accountants, engineers, homemakers, parents, managers, mechanics, drivers, pilots, designers, teachers, principals, business owners, entrepreneurs, and the many other roles through which

they can share your word, love, provision, and good news. And strengthen the ministries of the graduates and staff members of the school. We pray in the name of Jesus Christ. Amen.

April 3: Accounting. Dear God, our provider, who pours out more blessing to us than we have the rooms to store, we thank you for your generosity, for how you provide for the school and the needs of its students, staff, and volunteers. Help the school's finance committee and bookkeepers and accountants keep sound accounts and be good stewards of all you provide. Let the school's accounting be honest, accurate, and complete, so that the school exhibits transparency reflecting your own omniscience. No one hides anything from you. Thus, keep our public and private representations accurate, honest, and reliable, so that we can be not only good stewards of all you provide but also good reflections of you and your righteous character. We ask these things in Jesus' name. Amen.

April 4: Endowment Board. Father God, our Messiah and Savior, we thank you for giving the school an endowment to benefit students year to year, reducing tuition, securing the school's finances, and balancing the school's budget in difficult years. Yet we also thank you for the generosity, skill, wisdom, and oversight of the school's endowment fund board. You have blessed these endowment fund board members with the ability and commitment to produce more income out of the funds you have already attracted to the school. You honor wise stewards, those who put your resources to work to earn you profits back rather than burying your resources in fruitless soil. Help the endowment board to earn you abundant returns with what you bring to them for their stewardship. But also let them know that you honor their work and their own giving. We ask in the name of our Lord and Savior Jesus Christ. Amen.

> **Posture.** Prayer doesn't require any special posture. In prayer, we look inward and upward with the eye of the mind and soul, toward where God resides. Posture can help center us for that inward journey. For your daily school prayers, bend over and inward, kneel, bow your head, open your hands, close your eyes or look up, or take whatever other posture helps you turn toward God.

April 5: Accountability. Dear Heavenly Father, in whom we trust, to whom we give highest honor, and to whom we owe our very lives, we thank you for keeping your every promise. We thank you that you do not change, are not arbitrary, and are never capricious. We thank you for your consistency and rationality and reliability. Help every member of the school community be like you in those respects. Give the students your character for accountability. Make the students reliable in their studies, devotions, and responsibilities. Make them reliable in both the school and their homes. And help the teachers, staff members, school leader, school board, and volunteers also be accountable to the school, its students, and you. You love accountability, and so we love accountability, too. You are the rock, not the shifting sands. Help us to be like rocks, too. In the name of Jesus Christ we pray. Amen.

April 6: Minds. Holy Father, we honor and worship you this Spring day, as we watch your creation come alive with the Spring rains and warmth. Thank you for replenishing the soil and bringing forth new life. We ask today that you would attend to the minds of the school's students, facing so much worldly strife. Still the minds of the school's students where you would have their minds be still. Liven the students' minds where you would have their minds come alive. Point their internal eye and train their internal dialogue toward your character and your movement in the world, so that they may know you, follow you, and honor you. We want the minds of the school's students to be clear, strong, full of hope, and soon full of knowledge not only about your world but also about you. Give the students minds of hope, faith, and discernment. Show them the future you have for them in you. We ask in the name of our Lord Jesus Christ. Amen.

April 7: Givers. God our Father, today we celebrate your omniscience, your goodness, and your sovereignty. We thank you today for the givers of the school, from the students who share their joy and faith with other students

so generously, to the teachers who sacrifice their time and exhaust their energy to teach and encourage the students about you. We thank you today for the givers of funds, the givers of time, and the givers of talents who enrich and enliven and steady and bless the school. Draw together this community of givers in glorious celebration of you. Thank you above all for blessing the school's givers with the time, talent, energy, resources, and wisdom to share so generously with the school. In Jesus' name we pray. Amen.

April 8: Giving. Righteous Father, Glorious One, today is your day, as every day is your day. We thank you for the morning, the noon, and the evening. We thank you for giving us breath and another day to enjoy and serve you. Today we pray for joyous giving throughout the school. We know that you honor a joyful giver. The school has so many givers whose hearts are after you. Students give their devotion to you and their time and service to others. They give their will to obey you and the school's rules, and they give their honor and respect to their teachers and school leader. The school's teachers give their time, skill, and sensitivity to their students, their respect to their school leader, and their obedience to the school's mission. The school's board honors you in all it does, waiting patiently for your word and then governing according to your will. The school's volunteers give of their time and talents, and the school's donors give of their treasures. Let this day and every day of the school year be a day of giving, in honor of when you gave all by giving us your Son. We pray in his name Jesus Christ. Amen.

April 9: Bless God. Father God, your holy word exhorts us to bless you, which seems so strange, for you bless us so richly and so far beyond anything we can do for you. Yet because your word says that we should bless you, let every member of the school community do so today, endeavoring to find ways to bless you. Let the students bless you today by showing their obedience to your word. Let the teachers bless you today by showing to the students the teachers' desire to know you. Let the school leader bless you today by being to the school community the rock you are to us, stable, confident, and secure because standing on you. Let the school's volunteers bless you by serving the school richly, as you have served them, blessing them with the means to give back to you. May we bless you today, oh God. In Jesus' holy name we pray. Amen.

Story. When you pray, you are both recalling God's grand narrative and once again entering this story. You want your life to have purpose. It does so when you participate in God's grand narrative. Your daily school prayer is helping you do so.

April 10: Police Officers. Dear God, Our Father, we thank you for the protection of the local jurisdiction's police officers. We thank you for their devotion to duties and to ensuring that the school's students are safe from harm. We thank you when they direct traffic for student safety and for their swift response to emergencies and alarms. We thank you that they secure the school through criminal history checks, vandalism and trespass investigations, and safety inspections. We thank you that they keep a lookout to discourage others from even considering harming the students of the school. We ask that you protect the school's police officers from harm as they go about their important duties and that you bless them for their devotion to you and to the safety and security of the school. We most of all ask that they, like the school's students, would know, love, and obey you, so that they would have eternal life through your Son. We pray in his name Jesus Christ. Amen.

April 11: Reading. Heavenly Father, we thank you that you are our God of reason, that you have given us reasoning minds, having blessed us with your image. We thank you for giving us the capacity to think and speak, even to write to communicate to one another about you. We ask today that you would help the school's teachers and volunteers teach the students to read. Help the young students recognize their letters and words and learn to read aloud and silently so that they can read and understand more about you. Help the school's older students to read not just for understanding but for comprehension. Help the school's students to read more swiftly and surely, with greater confidence and ability to understand the author's intentions. And help them choose wise and righteous things to read so that they may have pure minds, hearts, and souls. Give us all a passion to read your holy word so that we may know, worship, and obey you. We ask in Jesus' name. Amen.

April 12: Board Officers. God our Father, we thank you for leading and guiding the school. We thank you for opening the hearts of the school's board members to accept the offer of board service. We also thank you for the wisdom, discernment, and governance they exhibit in honor of and obedience to you. We pray today for the board's officers, that they especially would hear, follow, obey, and honor you. Show them your movement. Show them your direction. Call them toward the tasks and duties you would have them do and toward the insights and revelations you would have them receive from you.

Show them your vision for the school so that the school toward which they govern is the school that still lies unformed in the future, ready to glorify you. Give them the faith that their discernment and decisions in obedience to you will lay the groundwork for your future for the school. We ask in Jesus' name. Amen.

April 13: Writing. Father God, whose Son Jesus Christ is the Word, we thank you for his revelation. We thank you for the minds you have given us to hear, read, understand, and follow your word. We pray today that you help the school's teachers guide the school's students in learning how to write, so that the school's students may communicate clearly in honor of you. You have given the school's students capacities that they do not yet even know they hold. With effort and sound instruction, many will become fine writers. Help all the school's students pursue the gifts they have for written communication. Help the school's students to hone their writing craft. And then give them your words to communicate, using holy and righteous communication that lifts others up in the way that you would have the students do. Strengthen the school's writing program, and raise up prophets, teachers, and preachers whose writings glorify you. We pray in Jesus' name. Amen.

April 14: Speaking. Heavenly Father, you spoke, and you created the world's order out of primordial chaos. You spoke, air separated from water, water from land, and night from day. You spoke, and plant life and animal life, and then human life in your image, arose. You spoke, and the prophets, teachers, kings, judges, disciples, and apostles recorded your words for us to read, treasure, obey, and share. And so, help the school's students to learn how to speak, both to speak well and to speak well of you. Help the teachers be sound instructors of the students in the students' private and public speech. Give the students the courage, confidence, and content to speak publicly in ways that honor you. And help the students to speak gently, sensitively, encouragingly, and truthfully, as your Holy Spirit moves and informs them to do. Also help the students to hold their tongues when you would have them not speak and never to speak ill of you. We pray in Jesus' name. Amen.

> **Unity.** In a distracted and fractious world, we spend a lot of our time in fragments. Our lives and identities are not whole. Prayer brings your fragments back into unity. Prayer makes you human and whole.

April 15: Singing. Lord God, your revelation tells us that heavenly throngs sing your praises continually to you. What joy and honor and privilege it must be to sing in your presence of your glory. And so help the school's students to carry those same songs in their hearts, minds, and souls, so that they would continually sing in praise of you. Help them to sing in school, at home, and in church, joyfully and confidently, knowing all that you have for them and all that you are to them, and knowing that their song pleases you. Don't let their songs be empty of love for you, just sounds, but instead let their songs come from their hearts out of pure and true devotion to you. Give them beautiful pitch and intonation, melodic and harmonious, so that their song honors your beauty. And give them the words to sing, too, words that honor and celebrate you. We ask in Jesus' holy name. Amen.

April 16: Family Churches. God our Father, maker of heaven and earth, who set us apart, calling us out in public assembly in these bodies we call our churches. The school's students and families belong to churches throughout the community. We pray today for those churches. Help the school's students and their families find sound churches with pastors who know how to guard their flock against false teaching and who give their lives for the flock. Help the school's students and their families worship devotedly, give generously and joyfully, and serve abundantly and with dedication in their churches. Help the local churches welcome the school's students, offering them sound spiritual instruction and a place of warmth, care, love, and security. And find ways in which to connect the school with the local churches, promoting the mission of the churches to foster relationships with you through your Son Jesus Christ, in whose name we pray. Amen.

April 17: Spiritual Struggles. Heavenly Father, whose presence we desire, whose heart we hope to share, and in whom we place our entire trust, we pray today for the spiritual struggles going on in the school and in the hearts, minds, and souls of the school's students, teachers, leader, staff, and volunteers. We pray that you would help each member of the school community perceive the spiritual struggle they face and turn to you to prevail in that struggle. Show us the powers and principalities with which we contend, and give us the courage, heart, and discernment to respond with your word, stance, and attitude to defeat those powers and principalities in your great battle your Son Jesus already won on the cross. Help every student and other member of the school community to turn to you and your word in our spiritual struggles, so that we may prevail as your Son has already prevailed for us. Let us be the victors you would have us be, so that we may honor and credit you for having defeated all enemies. In the name of our Savior Jesus Christ we pray. Amen.

April 18: Lost. Father God, we pray today for the lost souls of the school community, for those students, staff members, and volunteers who do not know that your Son Jesus Christ took his throne on the cross to pay for what they owe, or that he rose from death to defeat the death

they face. We ask that you would send us or send another to share with those lost souls this good news, this greatest news, that we can live eternally with you and in you, if we only accept our utter need for your Son's great sacrifice, in your grand plan to bring all humankind and all creation back to you, redeemed and resurrected through Christ's inestimable work on the cross. Give us a voice of gentleness, clarity, and conviction to speak your good news to those who need it. Soften their hearts to hear. For we know your desire that none be lost. In Jesus' glorious name we pray. Amen.

April 19: Elderly. Dear Lord, Our Father, we pray today for the elderly of the school community. The school has older retired teachers and staff members, older volunteers and former volunteers, and even older graduates and parents or grandparents of students and graduates. We love the elderly of the school community. We honor their service to you throughout their lives, with such dedication. We thank you for bringing them to the cross and encouraging them that they will have you in eternity. Help our elderly to run their race to its glorious end. Keep our elderly safe and strong for as long as you have a ministry for them here on earth, before calling them to heaven. And help us show them the love and respect, and to care for them, in the way that they deserve. We pray in the name of our Lord Jesus Christ. Amen.

April 20: Unborn. Heavenly Father, King of kings, Prince of peace, we pray today for the unborn children of the school community, region, nation, and world. We pray that you would strengthen and nourish them by strengthening and nourishing their mothers. We pray that you would help the mothers and fathers of the unborn to prepare their place for them in the world, supported, loved, cared for, protected, and desired. We pray that the unborn children and their mothers would endure a safe delivery so that both mother and child would be healthy. We pray that medical care would be available and effective, and that the post-natal care would be so, too. We also pray that no unborn child or pregnant mother would suffer demise. We know that you knit us together in the womb and have plans to prosper us. Let it be so. We pray in the name of our rescuer Jesus Christ. Amen.

April 21: Infants. Dear God, Our Lord and Savior, we marvel at the beauty and design of your creation, especially humankind, created in your image. When we see the infants whom you bring forth from their mothers, you stun us with their exquisitely delicate fingers and toes, and arms and legs, and their already profound eyes and face, in which we already see such incredible capacity. We pray today that you would help every parent of the school care for their infants, bringing them to maturity. We pray that every infant born in the school's families would come to know you and to receive the salvation and eternal security of your Son Jesus Christ. Help the school community to care for its families with infants. Surround the school's infants with love, concern, and care, and provide for the families who nurture infants. These things we ask in our Lord Jesus' name. Amen.

April 22: Mothers. Father God, Lord of all heaven and earth, thank you for the mothers of the school, for how they have persevered in childbirth and child raising to bring to the school their students for education in your way and purpose. Thank you for how you have blessed the mothers of the school with their family ministries, strengthened them for their precious duties, and given them the deepest capacity to love and nurture the school's students. Help the school and its teachers and students show the school's mothers the respect and honor they deserve and earn by caring so well for the school's students. Give the mothers due honor and place within the school community, so that they know that the school recognizes them and cares for them as they are well due. And strengthen the school's mothers in all they do for their families and the school's students. We pray in Jesus' name. Amen.

April 23: Fathers. Heavenly Father, glorious Son, and Holy Spirit, we think today of the school's fathers, those men who have sent their sons and daughters to the school for instruction in your word and way and in the purpose you have for them, which is to know you and join you in eternity. Thank you for the fathers of the school's students, for their faith, their service, their courage, and their generosity. Strengthen the school community's fathers for their family duties so that they may protect, guide, challenge, and encourage their students, without frustrating and exasperating them, but instead lifting them up for learning. Equip the fathers with the skills of raising strong, adventurous, and righteous children. And let the school community give due honor to the school's fathers for all that they do, especially for how they honor and serve you. We ask in the name of our Lord Jesus Christ. Amen.

> **Communion.** Prayer is communion with God. Yet prayer is also communion with others who pray for the same things. When you join your school community in daily prayer, you commune with other praying members. Your hearts and souls unite. Watch how your school community's corporate prayer unites.

April 24: New School Families. Dear God, our Holy One, our righteousness, we glorify and bless you today, remembering who you are and what you have done for us. We thank you today for the school's new families, for those parents who brought their students to the school for the first time this year or who have indicated their intention to send their students to the school next fall. Help the school's leader, administrators, teachers, and other staff members to welcome the new school families, orient them to the school's programs and activities, and encourage them in their choice of the school. Help the new families to find new friends and trustworthy teachers and staff relationships in the school. And help the families find their own ministries within the school as volunteers. Bless the school's new families, protect them, and help the school community to care for, love, and educate their students, fulfilling the parents' trust in the school. In the name of Jesus Christ our Lord we pray. Amen.

April 25: Athletics. Father God, we pray today for the school's athletics events and teams. We pray that you would hearten and strengthen the school's students through those sports and athletics events, that the students would learn to strive and compete and cooperate, in good sportsmanship while following the rules and giving it their best. Help the school's athletic director organize,

promote, and officiate safe and healthy athletic competitions and activities. Help the school locate, train, and compensate skilled and committed athletic coaches, assistance coaches, officials, and volunteers. Provide for the school so that it can acquire the facilities, grounds, uniforms, and equipment for the students to use and enjoy in athletic activities and competitions. Help the students to find their place on the playing floors and fields. And protect the students, coaches, and officials against injury. Let the athletic competitions and teams represent you well, winning and losing with grace, while showing competitors respect and even forgiveness for transgressions. In the name of our Lord Jesus Christ, we pray. Amen.

April 26: Strength. Dear Heavenly Father, we bless and glorify you today with every breath. We thank you for your creation and the place you have given us in it and even above it, for you have called us to steward and rule it in your will and way. We pray today that you would strengthen every member of the school community to do your will, beginning with the school's students. Give every student the vigor and capacity to strive after your desires, to learn, and to grow as you would have them do, to their full capacity to serve and love you. Give every teacher the strength to teach the students and serve the school. Give the school's leader the strength to direct the school, and the school's staff the strength to keep the school's operations orderly. Give the school's volunteers strength for their school duties, too. We need your strength to accomplish your desires. Give us the strength to endure. In the name of Jesus Christ, we pray. Amen.

April 27: World. Lord God, to whom every knee will bow and whose glory every tongue will confess, we thank you for your creation. We pray today that you would teach the students of the school about your creation and their place in it. Teach the school's students about the world, too, how you are redeeming it of its brokenness and corruption. Keep the students from falling to the world's ways, standing instead on your righteousness to work with you in redeeming the world. Guard the school's students against the world and its ways that lead to death and destruction. Redeem the school community and the world, with every member of the school community actively participating with you in that redemption, already accomplished on the cross but still ongoing to that day of your Son's return. We pray in his holy name. Amen.

April 28: Military. Dear Heavenly Father, we thank you for the protection you provide through the nation's military members. We thank you for giving the nation's military members and veterans the will, strength, and courage to serve so sacrificially, after the nature of your own Son Jesus Christ, to protect us. We ask today that you would protect the nation's military members against harm, reward them for their service, and call them to your kingdom quickly and securely if any should perish in their duties. We ask that you would help us to honor the nation's veterans and support the nation's military members, showing them the respect they deserve and ensuring that our government and communities provide for their due recognition and care. We further ask that you would heal those military members and veterans who have suffered injury or illness in their military service, so that they could lead fruitful lives once again. And protect and encourage the families of the nation's military members, while giving us the heart to care for the families who grieve over the loss of their member in military service. In Jesus' name we pray. Amen.

> **Honesty.** Our daily school prayers need not use traditional, pious language. Drawing on that language is fine. It follows a rich history. But heartfelt honesty is more important to prayer than a specific language. Yes, choose your words carefully in prayer. Yet also speak honestly.

April 29: Nation. Dear Lord God, we approach your throne today aware of the privilege it is to address you, to know you, to ask things of you, things we in no sense deserve but that you nonetheless desire for us in your mercy, expressed so fully when you sent your Son Jesus to the cross. In all humility, we pray today, as a school community, for the welfare of our nation and the discernment and courage of its leaders. Nations rise and nations fall. Do not let this time be a time of falling. We do not want our nation to fall away from you, bringing on us our rightful destruction. Instead, we want our nation to draw closer to you, to avoid its fall and destruction. We ask today that you would guide the nation's leaders to acknowledge and respect you, and to lead and serve as you would have them do, which is after your righteousness and depending on you. Forgive the nation its many debts, as you forgive us our many sins against you. And help the school's students to pray for the nation and participate in its call back to righteousness. We pray these things in the name of our Lord Jesus Christ. Amen.

April 30: Great Commission. Father God, you who spread the nations around the world following Babel's fall, and gave the nations over to powers and principalities from your realm, those powers having led the nations away from

you and astray, we ask today that you would call the nations back to you. Your Son gave us the Great Commission to make disciples of the nations. Help the school's students to learn their role in doing so. Help the school's teachers to instruct the students in your Great Commission and

how they can dutifully participate. We want to see the nations return to you, as your revelation expresses, for their redemption in your kingdom. We honor you for calling the nations back to you and declaring that they have a role and place in your kingdom. Let the school and its students participate fruitfully in your Great Commission. We pray in Jesus' name. Amen.

May 1: Struggles. Heavenly Father, the school community always has students who struggle. Students struggle with their growth, appearance, relationships, learning, homework, exams, and even their faith, confidence, and courage. Students struggle in school classrooms, hallways, and the gym, playgrounds, and cafeteria. They struggle meeting teacher expectations and following school rules. They struggle in their friendships and other peer relationships. We acknowledge that these struggles are appropriate for growth but also that some are due to rebellion, carelessness, selfishness, and sin. We pray today that the school would be effective in helping students persevere through and overcome their struggles, especially by relying on you and your word, while turning from their sin and forgiving the sins of others adversely affecting them. Help the school's students through their struggles, and let their struggles lead them to you. We pray in Jesus' name. Amen.

May 2: Fundraisers. Dear God, our provider, we pray today for the school's fundraisers, that the students, families, and volunteers of the school would seek the participation of others in the school's funding in appropriate ways. We pray that the school's administrators and teachers would choose the right fundraisers for the right reasons, and that students would participate in fundraising in ways that benefit their education, growth, and learning. Let the fundraisers succeed in their righteous purposes, to benefit the school and its students. Help the school apply the raised funds for the best benefit of the school's students. And don't let the fundraising burden any individual, student, or family inappropriately. We know that you hold everything in your hands and provide for all our needs. Do so as you see best through the fundraising efforts of the school. We pray in Jesus' name. Amen.

History. Prayer draws fruitfully on those who have prayed before you. Your prayer follows a profound history. Think of the Bible figures, Jesus most prominent among them, who prayed for you. When you pray, you draw on the history and tradition of their prayers.

May 3: Potential. Father God, our Lord, we come before your throne today mindful of the future of the school's students. We do not know what the future holds. Who can predict the future? But you know the potential that the future holds. Only you can bring things forth from nothing. Only you see the things that are truly possible for the students of the school. Help the students to respect their future. Help the students to sacrifice today for their future, the future of their own families, and the future of their classmates. Help the students plant the seeds today that will become their fruit tomorrow. Preserve and protect the future of the students, keeping them from harm and destruction that would steal their future. Show the students glimpses of their potential, in the schoolwork they complete, their athletic efforts, their student and teacher relationships, and especially their growing relationship with you. And give the students ambition to achieve, to expand and enjoy their futures, as they walk through life securely with you. We pray in Jesus' name. Amen.

May 4: The Lord's Prayer. Heavenly Father, as a school community, we pray the prayer today that your Son taught

us to pray. Help the school's students to learn, remember, and pray this prayer, with their whole hearts, knowing that Jesus gave it to us to pray. And so, our Father, who art in heaven, hallowed be thy name. Thy kingdom come, thy will be done, on earth as it is in heaven. Give us this day our daily bread, and forgive us our sins, as we forgive those who sin against us. Lead us not to temptation, but deliver us from evil. For thine is the kingdom and the power and the glory forever. Amen.

May 5: Return. Lord God, our Father, thank you for sending your Son into your creation, to reveal yourself through him and to redeem the world through his sacrifice on the cross and resurrection from death. We revel in his accomplishment, glorifying you and himself, while drawing all things together in him. When he ascended, you sent the promise that he would return and that after he returned, you would unite heaven and earth in your holy city. Help the school's students and school community to anticipate your Son's return. Help the students of the school to know that all things will end in glory. We pray that your Son's return would both be swift but also in due time, after everyone who would join you in your kingdom would have the opportunity to do so. Move the students' hearts and minds to make the good confession and receive your Holy Spirit, so that when your Son returns, all would join you for eternity. We pray in Jesus' name. Amen.

May 6: Models. Father God, we celebrate your wonders today, seeing the world you created, sensing the vastness of your universe, and trying to imagine your infinite, unconfined, and undefined power. We have no doubt of your ability to hear our prayer and to grant our prayers, nor doubting your desire to do so. Today, we pray that the school and its teachers would be able to present to the students models for their own behavior, knowing that your Son Jesus Christ will always be their ultimate and best model. Help the teachers and volunteers of the school be models for the students, exhibiting behaviors and attitudes that the students can responsibly imitate. Give the students models in their studies, from the arc of your own grand narrative. And let the students find model behaviors in their parents, grandparents, siblings, and neighbors, too. Help the school community to model the behaviors and attitudes you desire, command, and respect. In Jesus' name we pray. Amen.

May 7: Mentors. Dear Heavenly Father, we come before you humbly today, under the cleansing blood of your Son, with only his obedience as our justification. We thank you for giving us your Son to choose and instruct the first disciples and for the ministry with which you blessed those disciples, handed down to us now through two millennia. We ask for our prayer today that you would reveal to the students of the school willing mentors to disciple them in your way, especially over the coming summer. We know that the school's students need not just others to imitate but others to guide and coach them, to teach them how to navigate the unrighteous world righteously. Bring those mentors to the attention of the school's leader, teachers, and families, to connect students with them. Move the hearts of sound mentors to offer their time and insights to the school's students. Form strong and sound mentor relationships on which the students can depend. We ask this grace in the name of your Son Jesus Christ. Amen.

> **Listening.** God intends prayer to be communication. Communication implies both speaking and listening. Say your daily school prayers. But also listen. If your mind forms words, seemingly in response to your prayers, don't immediately reject those words as your own thoughts. They may instead be nudges from the Holy Spirit. Test those words. They may include God's answer.

May 8: Apprenticeships. Lord God, our Father, we who are your adopted children, who follow the path and glorious model of your Son Jesus Christ, we pray today that you would reveal to the school's students this summer fruitful apprenticeships, in which they can learn practical skills and crafts that will serve them, serve their families, and enrich the community, now and as they mature and move into the workforce and in forming their own families. Move the hearts of skilled individuals of good Christian character, to introduce the school's students this summer to vocations like home maintenance and improvement activities, vehicle maintenance and repair, design, decorating, sewing, cooking, gardening, and lawn care. Help the school, its teachers, and its families find jobs and duties the students can perform this summer that will improve their discipline, build their character, and build their skills, even while teaching them how to earn and manage money. These things we ask in Jesus' name. Amen.

May 9: Financial Literacy. Father God, we want the school's children to be responsible in all things including in how they steward the gifts you give them and income they earn and others earn and share with them. We pray today that the school would teach its students financial

literacy, whether in mathematics, social studies, home economics, or other courses, as a fitting and priority application of their learning. Equip the teachers, volunteers, and mentors of the school to communicate to the school's students the methods and significance of managing money well, so that they may tithe and offer to you, provide for themselves and their family, and be secure in times of want out of times of plenty. Teach them that borrowers are slaves to lenders and that a little folding of the hands brings want. Help them to receive, understand, and follow your many words on how they should relate to and manage money. We ask in Jesus' holy name. Amen.

May 10: Service. Dear Heavenly Father, our Creator and Savior, and through your glorious Son Jesus Christ also our brother and friend, although you are the creator and ruler of heaven and earth, you are also a servant, indeed your Son a suffering servant. We know that your heart is to serve and rescue more than to judge and condemn. Your Son Jesus Christ proved so on the cross. We thus pray today that the school's students would be servants after your heart, that they would find ways to serve one another, serve their teachers, serve the school, and serve their families. We marvel at the small and large acts of kindness and service we already see the school's student's doing. Give the school's students a larger heart for sacrificial service in the model of your Son's service, while letting them know that you see and appreciate their service even when others don't. And give the teachers and other members of the school community the same heart. We thank you for blessing the school with servant students, teachers, volunteers, and leaders. In Jesus' name we pray. Amen.

May 11: History. Lord God, who dwells in the highest heaven, yet stooped so low as to walk and talk with us, we will be forever in awe and in your debt for the radical act of love through which you set the course of history. We pray today that every student of the school would know your story and its history, especially the coming of your Son Jesus to confirm and complete the course of history. At the same time, we ask that you give the students a mind and passion for learning the history of your church and your people, and other history that will inform the students how to live and discern. Equip the school's teachers to share the significance and lessons of history, so that the school's students do not unwisely repeat it. And help the whole school community know its own history so that they may be confident in the place the school has in your story. We pray in the name of our Savior Jesus Christ. Amen.

May 12: Citizenship. God our Father, we thank you for offering us citizenship in heaven through the blood of your Son Jesus Christ. We value no citizenship more than to enter and dwell in your kingdom. Today we pray that you would help the school's students become and remain citizens of your kingdom, with their destiny beside you in heaven. We also pray that the school's students would become model citizens here on earth, obeying the just rules and laws of the community and nation to which they belong, and reflecting well on you through their contributions to the society in which they reside. Your disciples have been the bedrock of so many societies, freeing those societies of oppression, stabilizing them, and helping them to flourish. Shape the minds and hearts of the school's students so that they may be those citizens on whom communities and the nation depend to flourish under your loving rule. And let every other member of the school community do likewise, holding up your honor before others, as model citizens. In the name of your one and only Son Jesus Christ we pray. Amen.

> **Revelation.** You may have realized that prayer seems to occur at different levels, from the practical to the profound. Helpful prayer reveals your own character for your examination and repentance. The deepest prayer reveals God's character in transformative effect.

May 13: Government. Dear Heavenly Father, you whom we adore, knowing your goodness, depending on your righteousness, and receiving your provision and blessing, we pray today that the school's students would learn about not only your beneficent governance of creation but also of human government. Equip the school's teachers to show the students the necessity of sound government, the forms of sound government, and the results of sound government, along with the evil and oppression that can result under corrupt government and the Christian way to oppose and end those corruptions. Help the school's students to learn to relate responsibly to government so that they may not suffer the government's condemnation but may instead uphold, promote, and even participate and lead in sound government, while relieving the citizenry of government error, corruption, and oppression. And we ask that you do the same for every other member of the school community. We pray earnestly in our Lord Jesus Christ's name. Amen.

May 14: Leadership. Lord God, we credit you with giving us models for righteous leadership, especially the model of your Son Jesus Christ. We know the necessity and benefit of strong and sound leaders who have your Son's heart and receive the wisdom of the Holy Spirit. We also know the perils of corrupt leadership and the need to continually raise and train new leaders who have your heart and wisdom. We pray today that you would equip the school's teachers, volunteers, and families to make leaders out of the students whom you have chosen for that role. Help the school to give students opportunities to lead, roles of leadership, responsibilities of leadership, and leadership rewards. Make the school's students to be servant leaders in the way that your Son showed and your word teaches. Give the school's graduates the skills, heart, courage, and opportunity to lead families, businesses, charities, churches, communities, states, and nations. Foster the heart and offer the mantle of leadership to those students and graduates whom you choose. We pray in the name of your Son Jesus Christ. Amen.

May 15: Strangers. Father God, our lantern, light, and redeemer, we pray today that the school's students would learn from their teachers the right conduct and attitude toward strangers. We pray that the students would be wise and cautious in their contact with strangers, so that they suffer no harm. Yet we also pray that the students would not unduly fear the stranger or foreigner, for we know the heart that you have for the wanderer, outcast, and immigrant, finding many such prophets among your Bible figures, and knowing your own word and the model and parables of your own Son. Do not let the students or other members of the school community mistreat the stranger, foreigner, or immigrant, but rather to help them along their paths toward you. Help the students to discern properly the strange things they should avoid, born from dark arts and powers, while discerning and accepting the good and holy things that only look strange because of our own sin and corruption. For in that way, the school's students may welcome and entertain your own angels. In Jesus' name we pray. Amen.

May 16: Tribes. Heavenly Father, who recognized the twelve tribes of Israel, brought forth your Son from one of those tribes, and distinguish between righteous and unrighteous conduct and attitudes of tribes and their people, we pray today that you would help the school's students to understand both the healthy and potentially

unhealthy aspects of being members of tribes and their families. We want the students to love and respect their families and celebrate their national and ancestral heritage, so that they draw solace, community, and strength from their social context. But we also want the students to welcome, value, and respect members of other families and tribes, of different customs, culture, and national and ancestral heritage. Help the school and its students to celebrate their own tribes and heritages while welcoming other tribes and heritages. But above all, help the school and its students, teachers, leader, staff members, and volunteers to unify around you, over and above all tribes. We pray in Jesus' name. Amen.

May 17: Worldviews. Lord God, we thank you for giving us life, for giving us the means to sustain life, and for giving us lives in which we are capable of knowing and embracing you, our creator. We also thank you for your holy word. We learn from your word how distorted is our view of reality, your creation, and its true patterns, principles, and designs. We pray today that you would give the students of the school your view of creation and their place in it. Equip the teachers to show the students how other views of the world distort your true and sound view of your creation. Help the students recognize that culture, though necessary, will always distort your reality and that they must return to your word and seek your wisdom to see the world as it is. Help the students acquire the capacity to recognize worldviews, perspectives that both inform and distort, so that they can view the world and their place in it accurately, fruitfully, according to your word, and so that they may discern, judge wisely, and flourish. In Jesus' name we pray. Amen.

May 18: Loss. Father God, you know the pain and trauma of loss, having given your Son for our redemption. Your Son wept, showing your character for compassion. We pray today for the members of the school's community who have suffered loss, are grieving losses, and need your consolation and would benefit from the comfort of others. Help the school's students both recover from loss and show compassion for others who have suffered from loss. Comfort every member of the school community, from students to teachers, other staff members, families, and volunteers, who has suffered loss and grieves over their loss. Heal the wounds of loss, and give the grieving a new heart. Let the losses that students and other members of the school community suffer remind them that you are our comforter and that you rescue us from loss. And help us to look forward to joining you in heaven where no tears fall. In the name of our Lord and Savior Jesus Christ we pray. Amen.

> **Savoring.** Prayers pursue God's good. But our daily school prayers may do more than just ask God for more good. Our daily school prayers can also savor the good God has already done. Let your school prayer time include thanking God for the good already done and relishing in his goodness.

May 19: Heaven. Heavenly Father, our Wonderful Counselor, Almighty God, and Prince of Peace, we pray today out of a longing to join you in heaven. You have placed eternity in our hearts, so that we wish to cross that divide into your eternal kingdom. We pray today that you would give the students of the school a heart for heaven, that you would help the school's teachers, other staff members, and volunteers show the students your path to heaven through your Son Jesus Christ, and that every student would pursue that path, as you pursue us. Help the school teach the students about heaven and share the excitement and desire for heaven. Help the students store their treasures in heaven so that they may have eternal rewards for their earthly labors. Reveal aspects of your heaven to every member of the school community, so that their anticipation for entering heaven grows. We pray for these glorious things in the name of our Lord Jesus Christ. Amen.

May 20: Decisions. Lord God, you know the many decisions that the school's students, teachers, other staff members, leader, and volunteers face. You know how significant decisions can be. Help the school's teachers, other staff members, and volunteers equip the students to make good decisions, right decisions, decisions that honor you, fulfill your desires, and obey your word. Gently show the students how poor decisions, bad decisions, dishonoring decisions can lead to despair and destruction, but quickly restore the students from their errors so that they suffer no long-term harm and instead only learn their lessons. Also show the students the rewards of good and righteous decisions, especially those rewards that they store up in heaven, in your heart, honoring and glorifying you. Let the students' decisions bless them, their families, their teachers, and the school. Make sound discernment and good judgment a hallmark of the students of the school, both during their school years and on into their adulthood. In Jesus' name we pray. Amen.

May 21: Literature. Almighty God, we glorify, bless, and honor you today, thanking you for your goodness, provision, and salvation. We thank you especially today for your care and concern for the school for which we pray. Today, we ask that you help the school show its students the depth, breadth, and richness of literature, from the vast literature surrounding, exploring, and promoting your word, to the many other forms of literature that carry echoes and resonance of your beauty, intelligence, design, and glory. Open the hearts and minds of the students to literature so that they become lovers of your word and adventurers on your journey. Give them a desire to open the pages of books or to turn their screens toward literature. Equip the school's teachers to introduce students to the classics so that someday the school's students as graduates would be well read, especially appreciative of the profound literature informing the world of your presence and grand narrative in which we find our hope, purpose, and meaning. In Jesus' name we pray. Amen.

May 22: Student Blessing. Father God, we pray today that you would bless every student and graduate of the

school. We may have in mind certain students, perhaps our own children or grandchildren, students who currently struggle, or students who have touched our hearts in some way. But even if we have those students in mind, we pray for all students and graduates of the school. Our prayer is that you would know them, love them, draw them, and ensure that they join you in your kingdom. Our prayer is that you would protect them, guide them, challenge them, restore them when they fall, and heal them when they suffer. Our prayer is that you would hold them in your heart, lift them with your hand, shelter them under your wing, and breathe your life into their lungs so that every breath they take they remember and honor you. Keep the school's students precious in your sight. Forgive them their wrongs, redeem them from corruption, and lead them in paths of righteousness. Bless their families as well. We ask in Jesus' name. Amen.

> **Symphony.** When you pray daily along with your school community, your prayers raise a symphony to God. Each of you pray with a different voice, tone, tenor, and passion. Imagine how that variety sounds to God.

May 23: Boundaries. Heavenly Father, we draw near to you today with concern for the school's students, they that would know the boundaries beyond which you would not have them pass and that they would respect those boundaries. You made us creatures of free will, granting us not only the power to choose but the knowledge of what you desire and command that we choose. You forbid us from things that would only harm us, while granting us all that is good. Help the school's teachers to instruct the students in proper boundaries for their personal conduct. Help the school's administrators support the teachers in the proper and merciful enforcement of those boundaries so that students would learn of consequences without suffering harm. And help the school's families support the school in the boundaries the school sets and enforces mercifully, justly, gently, and only for shaping the good character of the students. Give the students discernment for your boundaries and the desire to obey you in respecting those boundaries. We pray in Jesus' name. Amen.

May 24: Company. Blessed Father, our Holy God, we cherish your presence and seek your company. We also cherish the fellowship of believers, among whom we form and constitute your body, your Son's bride, the church. We pray today that you would help the students of the school keep good company. Equip the teachers to show the students what good company means, how good company holds students accountable to good behavior, and how bad company corrupts. Keep the students from choosing bad company and being bad company from others. Help the students to make good choices of friends and among friends, so that their groups encourage their members in good behavior. Give students the discernment to recognize bad company and the dangers that bad company presents, and the courage to keep themselves apart from bad company. Show the students their own errors so that they may repent of those sins and become good company rather than bad company. These things we pray in the name of Jesus Christ our Lord. Amen.

May 25: Factions. Lord God, we humbly submit today to your rule, hoping to discern your will and pursue your desires. We pray today for the healthy interactions of the school's students, that they would avoid factions and cliques, and instead support one another, whether they belong to one another's grade, team, club, or other circle of friends. Help the school's staff members to guide the students into a healthy school culture, absent of bullying, hazing, and other forms of isolation, oppression, harassment, or intimidation. Help the school's teachers and administrators to correct any such misconduct firmly, swiftly, and mercifully, restoring offending students into good relationships with one another, their teachers, and the school. Give the students confidence in their relationship with and identity in you so that they do not form unhealthy factions and cliques in vain attempts to feed their insecurities. We want the school to reflect your kingdom. We ask these things in the name of our Lord Jesus. Amen.

May 26: Patterns. Our Father, we stand before your throne today marveling once again at the design and patterns of your creation. We see how you have ordered your creation from on high, with your highest thoughts forming the seed for the rest of creation, which thus takes your pattern. We ask today that the school's students would see your presence in creation, out of its beauty, order, magnificence, and splendor, and in the way your creation provides for us. Help the teachers to show the students your principles and patterns, and how you have woven those patterns into every aspect of creation. Help the students not only to recognize your design, principles, and patterns but also to follow your will, so that their own lives may reflect your character and goodness. Help the school to form and follow patterns, routines, and practices that honor you and attract others into your kingdom. Let the school's patterns, schedules, habits, and practices become rituals that align the school's students and staff with your design and desire for ordered liberty. We ask these things in the name of our Lord and Savior Jesus Christ. Amen.

May 27: Thanks for the Year. Father God, whom we adore and worship, and to whom we owe everything, we celebrate the nearing end of the school year. We thank you for everything you have done for the school and its students, families, teachers, leader, staff, and volunteers this year. We thank you for every answered prayer. We thank you that you went far beyond our prayers to do good things we had not even asked of you, out of your love for

the school's students and your desire that they would learn. We thank you for every new discovery of your creation that the students discerned, every new thing they learned about themselves and their proper place in your kingdom and in your creation, and every new thing they learned about their relationship with you. We thank you for the school and every member of the school community. You are a God of mercy and grace. You gave us this year far more than we deserved or earned, out of your goodness. We credit you with every accomplishment this school year. In the name of Jesus Christ we pray. Amen.

May 28: Teacher Recovery. Heavenly Father, as we near the end of the school year, we think of how diligently the school's teachers worked this year, thanking you for giving them the energy, health, persistence, and devotion to serve the school and its students so well. We pray today that you would give the teachers rest and recovery on their break this summer from teaching. Keep them from illness and injury this summer, instead giving them relaxation and refreshment where they most need it, so that they return next fall restored to teach effectively and energetically next school year. For those teachers desiring summer work, give them that desired ministry. For teachers hoping to improve their teaching knowledge and skill this summer, give them the means to do so. For teachers hoping to engage in new recreations or travel, or form new friendships, provide them with those opportunities. And for teachers hoping to spend time with their families, give them the time and memories they pursue. We ask these many things in the name of our Lord and Savior Jesus Christ. Amen.

May 29: End of School Year. Lord God, our peace and rest, your school anticipates its summer break with excitement and relish. Help the school's teachers, leader, staff, and volunteers to end the school year strong, equipping the students for a fruitful summer of rest, restoration, and exploration. Let the students have the energy and discipline to finish their assignments and exams. Ensure that every student has the health and vitality to do their best to meet grade and graduation requirements to advance to the next level. Do not let students fall behind at the end of the year and face having to repeat courses or a grade or miss graduation. Help the teachers finish their grading with the integrity and skill that will most benefit the students and encourage and guide their families in supporting the students' continued development. Bring joy, the sense of accomplishment, and the sense of satisfaction to the students and other members of the school community here at the end of the year. In Jesus' holy name we pray. Amen.

May 30: Fall Enrollment. Heavenly Father, we pray today for the school's fall enrollment, that you will bring the right number of students back to the school, filling the school's hallways and classrooms with exciting energy, and allowing the school to fulfill its mission of educating minds and shaping hearts to serve you in your glorious creation. Keep the commitment of the school's families strong this summer so that parents remain excited about their students' new school year next fall. Ensure that the school has the enrollment to meet its budget requirements to employ the skilled teachers and staff the school needs to carry out the school's educational mission. Help the school's teachers and administrators encourage the school's families about next fall here at the end of the school year. In Jesus' name we pray. Amen.

May 31: Summer Break. Father God, we pray today for the school's students on their summer break from school. Protect the students from illness, injury, and other harm this summer so that they can return to school in the fall rested and ready to learn more of you and your desires and your creation again next school year. Help the school's families give the students rich opportunities for growth this summer, even as the students relax and recover from the arduous studies of the past school year. Help the school, its students, and families also find relaxing but fruitful explorations this summer that will preserve and amplify what they learned in school this past year, whether those explorations may be reading, journaling, visiting libraries and museums, making things, working with other adults on projects, or learning new sports and recreations. Over the summer, let the students form and enjoy new friendships and find new models and mentors, too. Also give the students opportunities to travel, to explore their city, town, region, country, and world. Bring the students back to school next fall happy, refreshed, grown in their capacities, and ready for the new school year. In Jesus' name we pray. Amen.

Finishing Strong

Well done, good and faithful servant. You may already have seen evidence of God's gracious answer to your prayers. Or the evidence may only become clearer to you later, whether next year or in many years. Such are the rewards of teachers and school administrators and volunteers. Often, one doesn't hear the appreciation or see the results until a former student stops you in the grocery store years later, grown and matured into a life of flourishing. Don't fret over evidence, though. Our far greater rewards are in the eternal, heavenly realm. You won't truly see what God accomplished through your prayers until you see transcendently, as only one can do in his realm.

So, keep praying. Keep storing up treasures in heaven. And keep opening heaven's doors for God's mighty work. When his Son rose, God redeemed earth and heaven. Our privilege is to participate in that already accomplished but not yet fully realized work. Prayer is our divine purpose, that for which God created us, to revel in his desire to do the good that we ask from him when our motives are to honor, worship, and abide in him. A thousand celestial beings hear and celebrate your daily school prayer, when their divine Sovereign sends them forth to accomplish what you ask.

And even as you pray, row for shore. Let your prayers for your school community include your refreshed heart and new willingness to serve the school. God's answer to your prayer may be to nudge you in the direction of what he would have you do for the school. God may do as you pray without you having to lift a finger. What you ask of him may be something only he and others whom he motivates and equips can do. But he may instead provide you with the boat and oars against which to strain to bring your school cargo, the school's very students, to a safe shore. Or he may desire that you pull against the oars to draw his boat into deep waters, where students may fish for his profound truth.

Thus, pray for others in the school community, so that they may heal, serve, give, lift up the school, and solve the school's problems. But also let your prayer open your heart to see God's path for you, including a path of service to the school and its students. After all, God served you more abundantly than you'll ever be able to return, other than to give your own life to him, which is exactly what he hopes you will do. For in giving your life to him, through prayer and acts of submission, devotion, and service, you will have gained infinitely more back, including eternity. May God bless you while also blessing your prayers.

About the Author

Nelson Miller prays out of God's grace, informed by his experience as a husband, father, grandfather, Christian and public charter school board president, church operations director and band member, nonprofit board president, web content writer, and award-winning lawyer, law professor, and law school dean. He is the author of over eighty books on faith, law, and other subjects.

Faith Books by Crown Management, LLC

Spiritspeak: Sharing Some Very Good News | Gospelspeak: The New Testament | Biblespeak: The Epistles | A Letter to Memphis: Out of Egypt Reading the King's Text | The Faithful Lawyer | Answered Prayers: Conversations with the Living God | Secret Devotion: Pursuit's Cure | Looking to Jesus: Thinking More Often and Deeply of Christ | Following Jesus: What He Said to Do, and What He Did | Gospel Stories: Reading Aloud About God's Kingdom | Pierce's Cause | Facing Death: Worthwhile Reflection on a Necessary Subject | Epic Good News: A Poem of Our Divine Universe | Walking Through the Bible: A Journey Guide | Your Reason for Being: Discovering Your "Why I Am" and "What Is My Purpose" | Top 100 Questions Asked Christians: Answers to Common Faith Concerns | Applying the Bible: Discipleship Exercises for Everyday Life | Living Scripturally from A to Z | Church Policies & Procedures: Common-Sense Guides for Administering Churches in a Complex World | Letters to America's Churches: Contemporary and Timeless Issues | Without Bars: Christian Poetry for Prisoners | What Just Happened: The World's Madness in Poetry | Bible Lands: A Tour of Scriptural Israel

www.ingramcontent.com/pod-product-compliance
Lightning Source LLC
LaVergne TN
LVHW041841070526
838199LV00045BA/1386